SURVIVAL TIPS FOR MUMS

PRACTICAL IDEAS FOR THRIVING IN THE EARLY YEARS OF MOTHERHOOD

BY

ELIZABETH EL MOSTAIN

EP BOOKS (Evangelical Press)
Registered Office: 140 Coniscliffe Road, Darlington, Co. Durham, UK DL3 7RT

www.epbooks.org
admin@epbooks.org

EP Books are distributed in the USA by:

JPL Books
www.jplbooks.com
orders@jplbooks.com

and

10ofThose Ltd
www.10ofthose.com
sales.us@10ofthose.com

First published 2019

British Library Cataloguing in Publication Data available

ISBN 978-1-78397-287-6

I wish someone had given me this book when I was just embarking on the adventure of motherhood. It manages to be positive without being dewy-eyed. It is funny, warm, honest and Christ-centred and in addition is superbly practical about everything from the indignities of pregnancy, childbirth and breastfeeding to the annoyances of nits and everlasting laundry. And yet it is neither prescriptive nor preachy, just very readable and helpful.

Ann Benton, author

Reading *Survival Tips for Mums* is like having a friend who's parenting alongside you, who can encourage you when you need a nudge in the right direction, help you through the challenges and remind you of the positives, particularly of the many blessings there are—even if sometimes they feel buried under the responsibilities of parenthood, nappies, the ironing pile ... As you read, mums of young children will often find yourselves saying, 'so it's not just me!' Learn from an ordinary mum who's been there and learnt many helpful lessons along the way. Learn how to do family life well, by doing it as simply as possible. You will see that motherhood is a high calling—even if it's often lacking in glamour—or a wage. It's about learning to be a mum by grace, rather than by 'mumsnet'. These 'tips' are soaked in wisdom from God's Word, and show that even for busy mums, it's not just possible, but vital to keep in touch with God, and to live with His perspective—the wisest tip of all.

Julia Jones, Director of Women's Courses at London Seminary and supporting missionaries with Grace Baptist Mission

How does a mum of five children, pregnant with her sixth, find time to write a book? The answer is because she has lived what she writes and shares her fresh experience. Reading the book is like listening to Elizabeth chat about her reflections on being a busy mum over a cup of coffee. You will nod your head in agreement, smile as you picture her interacting with the children and grab a pencil to note down her wise advice.

Elizabeth is a young, lively, godly woman, living in the south of France, involved in mission work alongside her husband in a growing church. She writes with realism, honesty and frankness. You won't feel judged but rather inspired to persevere when you feel discouraged. You will be encouraged to care for yourself in every way as you are committed to loving your children well and creating a happy, healthy and God-honouring home. This book will give you fresh perspective and you will not only survive but thrive in the privileged role God has given you of being a mum. I can already think of many mothers to whom I would like to give this book.

Elinor Magowan, Pastor's wife, Women's Ministry Coordinator for FIEC, formerly UFM Women's Pastoral Worker.

Ever felt a little daunted when you hear about people like 'the young pastor's wife, living in a foreign country, speaking fluent French, bringing up six beautiful children' and you picture a 'perfect super-mum' who has it all together? The Proverbs 31 woman in person? Elizabeth's book blows this idea right out of the window as she shares her own struggles in learning the task of motherhood as we all do, one child at a time, one day at a time. It's a practical peek into her own home, amusing in places, but focused throughout on the grace of God in sending Jesus Christ, who, in redeeming us, also transforms every part of our lives. Elizabeth's informal style makes it feel like you're having a chat over coffee with an understanding friend, and its helpful layout means you can refer back to sections easily. It also oozes the wealth of sanctified common sense handed down from her own mother, something many young mums, including myself, wish we'd had.

I read it as a grandmother now, and would recommend it to all mums, because for all sorts of reasons, we all have those days when we struggle. This book takes us beyond surviving to thriving: physically, mentally, socially and spiritually. It doesn't send us on a parenting guilt trip but helps us in the wonderful privilege of introducing our little ones to the God who forgives, cleanses and restores us into a loving relationship with him. 'He remembers that we are dust', but sometimes we forget it, and comparing our perfect ideas of what we expected 'mummyhood' to be like, with the daily reality of what we are experiencing, destroys our confidence and our joy. This lovely book helps us to avoid that temptation and keep our sanity and enjoyment in raising the children God has blessed us with.

Colette Harding, Pastor's wife, mother and grandmother

This is the kind of book that would be great to give to any expectant or new mum as well as those who want to remember what it is like having little ones, so they can better help and encourage mums in their church. Like the title suggests it is very practical, full of helpful tips and advice—from keeping spiritually healthy to what high chair is best to buy! But it is also interspersed with lovely relatable anecdotes that serve to show a glimpse of what Elizabeth's home and children are like and the chaos that can sometimes be found (like lollies dripping down table legs). I found it very reassuring and honest! I wish it had existed when I first started parenting but I have three small boys at home and am thankful for the advice I can use now and some of the tips for situations I haven't experienced yet. I can imagine pulling this book back out when I face those challenges, like the children getting chicken pox! With so much choice and so many voices in the world telling Christian mums what is best, it is helpful to have an experienced and godly mum share what she has found work and encourage mums to keep on keeping on in Jesus.

Sibyl Brady, Pastor's wife and mother of three small boys

Contents

Mum Diary: October 2018
Sleep deprivation?
Today I arrived at my appointment with a midwife and realised with horror that I was still wearing my slippers. I tried to hide my feet with my bag in the waiting room.

To my sister Rosie, who is about to embark on the exciting journey of motherhood, and to my own mother, Alison, who taught me a lot of what is in this book without even realising.

Acknowledgments

Thank you ...

... to my kind husband for believing in this work and encouraging me at every step. I am blessed to be on this parenting journey with you and I couldn't wish for a better father for my children.

... to my six little treasures who inspire, love and challenge me every day. Thank you for letting me include the funny things you said when you were younger. I'm looking forward to the next ten years.

... to Dr. Alisha Symons for reading the manuscript and checking the medical side of things. I am so grateful to you and Brahim, Noémie and Léia, for your friendship and the adventures we have had together. Lakes, rivers, mountains, heatwaves, hurricanes, rain, mud and floods. Whatever next? I am glad that you always have spare socks, gloves and food in your car. Thank you for making every day we spend with you feel like a holiday.

... to Rosie, Colette and Elinor for checking the manuscript and giving me helpful ideas.

... to Serena, Lizzie, Lydia and Geoff. I would never have

turned my ten little ideas into a book without your encouraging comments.

... to all the Christian mothers and others who have influenced me over the years or helped us in practical ways. This book is really a collection of things that you have taught me.

... to all at EP for taking this book forward and being a pleasure to work with.

... to our Creator, Father and Saviour, for giving us life and for opening the door to eternal life. May you receive all the glory!

Introduction

From the moment you watch with bated breath while two little pink lines appear on the pregnancy test, your life will never be the same again. When I was pregnant with our first child we were living in a cosy little flat above the church where my husband was the assistant pastor. The kitchen had large windows looking out on a row of terraced houses, but all the other rooms had sloping ceilings, beams in funny places and only long horizontal slits to let light in. I put some pretty curtains over a low alcove to prepare a 'room' for our new baby. An elderly couple from church lived in a flat under ours and we shared a common staircase. They liked to have their heating on high and the warmth would waft up the stairs to us. I used to drape my washing over the banisters on a complicated assortment of hangers attached to airers. It dried in no time.

The days following the birth of a new baby are a strange and wonderful mix of joy, pain, exhaustion, excitement and change. When our baby was born, the flat was soon bursting with cards, flowers, presents and visitors—our church was full of very loving people. Someone wrapped pink ribbons around the railings outside. I remember the intense joy I felt throughout that first week even though, physically, I was in a mess. I would look at my baby and think, 'Wow, I did it. I actually gave birth.' I had an episiotomy during the delivery, followed, of course, by a good number of stitches. It was a bad idea for me to be walking around making tea for visitors, but I did it nevertheless and subsequentially got a painful infection in the wound. I struggled to position the baby for breastfeeding and had bleeding, cracked nipples. She was not getting enough milk because of difficulty latching on, so she cried all the time. I also wasn't wrapping her up warmly enough because I was trying to follow some advice that I had read about numbers of layers, rather than trusting maternal instinct. I had a total of eleven hours sleep in five days and my husband didn't get much more. I remember the midwife coming to see us and asking, 'Don't you have any windows you can look out of?' She wanted me to put my jaundiced baby in the sunlight, so I moved the moses basket into the kitchen.

On day five, my mum arrived, which was when things started to improve. She made me lie down with my knees up to let the episiotomy wound heal. She cooked delicious dinners and held the baby while I ate them. She wrapped the baby up warmly and bought a curtain to block off the draught from the corridor at the cold end of the flat. I started taking antibiotics for the infection. The midwife who had been visiting me went on holiday and a wonderful new midwife arrived exactly one week after the birth. She showed me how to position my baby so that feeding wouldn't hurt. I had to go back into hospital for three days with our daughter because she was dehydrated and needed intravenous fluids. The Sunday church service was just coming to an end as the new midwife left. My mum went downstairs and asked the preacher to announce a message from the midwife: 'No visitors for a week!' Through all of this,

I was full of joy despite the tears. I had a clear sense that God was looking after us and we would be okay. And we were.

When my eldest daughter reached the age of ten, already nearly as tall as me and barely recognisable as the fragile, dehydrated baby I had cried over a decade ago, I decided to celebrate ten years of motherhood by sharing ten 'mummy survival tips' on Facebook. I was surprised at the positive reaction they received and various comments that I should write a book. Well, here it is! This book will not tell you how to raise children in a godly way. There are already many excellent books on biblical parenting available. I have noted my personal favourites in the resources section on page 168, along with other books and websites that you may find helpful. This book will also not tell you how to organise your home, though it does inevitably touch on these things. Neither will it answer all your motherhood dilemmas. There are many things I don't cover as I have never had, for example, a caesarean section, a tongue-tied baby or a teenager. It is written from, and therefore limited by, my personal experience.

I grew up in London before heading to Aberystwyth University to study Fine Art and French. During this time, I met my husband on a French-speaking beach mission in Belgium. I was immediately struck by his love for the Lord, his sincere prayers, his ability to interact with children and his broad shoulders. We were married two years later. God has given us four daughters, one son and there is another little one on the way as I write. Two of our children were born in England and three in France. My husband has been the pastor of a small French church since 2010. Although we were both sent out as missionaries through the organisation United For Mission (UFM), I have always considered my main role to be that of supporting my husband in his highly specific calling, taking care of the home front in order to free him up for ministry. While I am very involved in the life of our church, in practical terms I am a full-time mother and homemaker. I was six weeks pregnant with our third child when we packed our boxes and moved across the channel. When our son was born, I had a three-year-old and a seventeen-month-old who was not yet walking. Learning to be a mother of three in a new country, far from the support of family, was extremely challenging. For about a year there often seemed to be at least one child crying. Over the last ten years I have always had at least one child in nappies, normally two, sometimes three. Finding easier ways of doing things has been a constant goal.

While my perspective on what it means to be a mother comes from the Bible, much of what I share in this book is not about right or wrong. God's unchanging Word gives us timeless wisdom on how to be good parents. The Bible's underlying principles of the value of motherhood can always be relied on, but the way we live these out will look different in each generation and culture. Whether you wean your baby by feeding him purées or go down the fashionable baby-led weaning route, is not a question of moral absolutes. Beware of books that try to make spiritual issues out of subjects that are actually cultural preferences. God is a God of abundance and choice. He has given us imaginations, creativity and the freedom to choose between different ways of doing things in many aspects of life. Your newborn will not be doomed to a life of self-gratifying disobedience if you decide to demand-feed him instead of schedule feeding. Neither will he grow up to become a rigid, legalistic or emotionally insecure character because you use a feeding schedule. The practical tips I give come from the viewpoint of a European, 21st-century Christian mother. Some of these tips will no doubt be out of date in

Europe in a few years and may not work in other cultures even now. So please don't feel that you must put everything that I say into practice. Each child is unique. What works with one may not work with another. It is not my intention to judge people who do things differently.

This book is divided into two parts. The first part looks at ways in which mothers can take care of themselves mentally, physically, spiritually and socially so that they are better equipped to serve their families. Motherhood requires us to pour ourselves out for the good of others, but you can't pour anything out of an empty bottle. When the Son of God came to earth as a baby to be our Saviour, he grew in a balanced, healthy way. 'And Jesus increased in wisdom [mentally] and in stature [physically] and in favour with God [spiritually] and man [socially]' (Luke 2:52). It is good to keep an eye on your children to assess how they are developing in these four areas,[1] but you need to make sure that amidst all the demands of daily life with small children, you also make time to fill up your own tank. Looking after yourself in these four areas will help you to look after your family. I am not promoting a Christian-coated version of worldly self-centredness. The world tells us to look out for ourselves first and foremost. 'Me-time' is a popular expression, while adverts tell us to indulge ourselves 'because we're worth it.' Let's be clear from the start, those who follow Christ are called to deny themselves, take up their cross and follow Jesus (Matthew 16:24). Faithfulness as a mother (or in any other calling) will involve suffering which no amount of practical advice can remove. My aim in giving ideas to help you thrive is not to encourage self-preservation for its own sake, but rather to equip you to continue living in sacrificial

1 See Ann Benton, *Aren't They Lovely When They're Asleep: Lessons in Unsentimental Parenting* (Christian Focus, 2007).

love for God's glory, over the long haul, instead of facing burnout at the first hurdle.

The second part of the book provides an A–Z of practical tips and ideas to help you in the daily tasks of being a mum. Motherhood is an adventure. I still have a long way to go and a lot more to discover. I don't always have it all together. There are still times when I lock myself in the bathroom and cry. I have, however, learnt some things which have helped me to survive the journey so far, during what is sometimes called the 'heavy-lifting' stage of parenting, and it is those things that I want to share in this book. I hope that you will find some of them helpful too.

Part 1
Tips for looking after yourself

1 Looking After Your Mental Health

The 'baby-brain' phenomenon is very real for many pregnant women and mothers of small children (but don't expect me to try to explain the science behind it!). My sisters-in-law and I all agreed recently that since having children we find it harder to focus on sermons and deep theological books. We are more prone to forgetting things because our minds are so full of juggling the practical needs of our families. It is said that mothers gain in empathy because, from the moment a baby is conceived, they no longer have just their own life to consider, but are responsible for the care of another little human being. Since having children, I have had to avoid watching the news too often. It actually hurts to see stories about children suffering. Motherhood certainly changes our outlook on the world and many aspects of how our minds and emotions work. Here we will consider some of the mental challenges that affect us as mothers and look at ways in which we can maintain our mental health.

Talk to an understanding adult

'I'm just not enjoying life much at the moment,' I said to my husband, looking sadly at my chopping board. The tears that fell were not because of the onions. Once again, I'd hardly had any sleep. Our five-week-old daughter had her days and nights back-to-front.

It is normal to feel tired, overwhelmed and a bit depressed at various times in the months following the birth of a new baby. Your body and lifestyle have undergone a massive upheaval. Your hormones are all over the place and if your baby is not letting you get much rest you are bound to feel emotional. You had so looked forward to becoming a mother, but now all you want to do is sleep! Telling a friend about how you feel can help a lot, but if you feel constantly negative and despairing about life and are struggling with everyday tasks or are losing interest in your baby, do speak to a healthcare professional about it. Postnatal depression is very common. It does not mean that you are a bad mother or that you will never feel better, but your body and mind may need some help during this difficult transition period.

Sometimes in the year following the birth of a new baby, I have gone through periods where I am so exhausted that if I talk to anyone in the evening, I burst into tears without even knowing why. Many of us can also feel like this around the time of our periods. It is sometimes better to just tell yourself to go to bed rather than crying down the phone to your mother and leaving her feeling like you are falling apart. You will probably feel brighter in the morning and if you do still need to talk to someone about your situation and feelings, you will be able do it in a more rational way. 'Weeping may tarry for the night, but joy comes with the morning' (Psalm 30:5).

Enjoy the good things

Taking the time to be thankful for the good things God has given you and allowing yourself to enjoy them can greatly help how you feel. Notice and appreciate the beauty in small things. We will talk later about the ways in which motherhood teaches us to make sacrifices for others, but I suspect that most women reading this are not in danger of selfishly living it up while their children are neglected. It is far more probable that caring mothers, in their good desire to serve their families, will fall into unsustainable patterns of self-neglect. Neither hedonism (living for pleasure) nor asceticism (denying yourself legitimate pleasures) are healthy extremes. Forgetting to appreciate the good things because you are weighed down with chores and just trying to get through the day, can lead to despondency and burnout. Motherhood is a marathon, not a sprint. We need to pace ourselves if we want to keep bringing glory to God through serving our families well for many years to come.

I remember dashing up the road to a medical appointment shortly after the birth of our third child, racing the clock as I panted along behind the double pushchair. My route led through a pretty town-centre square where people were sitting outside in the morning sunshine, enjoying hot drinks and relaxing. I felt so detached from their world, as if I belonged on another planet. How did anyone have time to sit around drinking coffee? Did people really do that? I was anaemic and felt snowed under by the demands of three tiny children. Warning bells now go off in my head when I start picturing myself as a rubber band that has been stretched too far and is about to snap, or an empty shell, drained and emotionless. My recovery began that summer when I decided to slow down and allow myself time to enjoy God's blessings. I swam in the sea and rediscovered what it was like to spend some time just having fun.

We live in a sin-damaged world where sickness, pain, tiredness, frustration and bad news often wear us down. Christians know that God has promised to make even these trials work for the ultimate good of his people (Romans 8:28), but God has also given us many obvious blessings and glimpses of his love. 'Every good and every perfect gift is from above, coming down from the Father of lights' says James 1:17. Make a conscious decision to enjoy rainbows, birdsong and spring flowers; trips to the beach, ice-cream and long chats on warm summer evenings; crunchy autumn leaves, steaming mugs of soup and firework shows; snowball fights, clear starry skies, a cosy blanket, hot chocolate and cuddles. Psalm 104 talks of God providing 'wine to gladden the heart of man, oil to make his face shine and bread to strengthen man's heart' (Psalm 104:15). Whether or not you drink wine or put oil on your face, the point here is that God doesn't just give us the bare minimum. His creation overflows with colourful gifts from our kind and wonderful Designer and Father. Many of these things can be enjoyed for free. Enjoying the good things with thankfulness can lift your spirits and help you to endure the hard stuff.

> Mum Diary: July 2013
> **Self-defence?**
> Today L caught a dragonfly and named it 'Potty.' Unfortunately, Y (age 2½) came along and squashed Potty. When asked why he did such a thing, Y's serious answer was, 'That dragon's eating me!'

Use your talents

I love the universe of small children, which is one reason why I keep having babies. There is nothing quite like the wonder of tiny hands and ears, a toddler's joy and amazement at the little things of life, the cuteness of miniature shoes and clothes, the sweet innocence of books and songs for babies, or their love for and dependence on mum for everything.

However, as much as we may love babies, it can be hard being surrounded all day by children, CBeebies and 'Baa Baa Black Sheep'. To keep things balanced, talk to adults whenever you can, read grown-up books about things that interest you and talk to your children about them, watch documentaries, go and discover new places with your children and use your talents to bless your family and others. Don't believe the feminist lie that you will somehow be less fulfilled if you prioritise being a wife and a mother. You may have given up a job that you loved in order to devote more time to your family. If you were a rocket scientist, it may be hard to find an outlet for this talent while at home with your children, but many of your unique skills and interests can still be developed and put to good use right where you are. This can stop you feeling like your brain is stagnating in a preschool world. Maybe you have a gift for encouraging others and can visit lonely people with your baby. Maybe you love baking and can develop that talent by making fantastic birthday cakes. Perhaps DIY is your thing, or gardening or crochet or car maintenance. You don't have to be good at everything. Avoid the trap of comparing yourself to others, or worse still, to Pinterest. Sure, use websites for getting ideas on how to store those bikes in a tidy way, but don't let yourself become riddled with guilt because you didn't make your own butter or hand sew all your baby's clothes! Develop your own set of hobbies and talents.

Of course, there will be periods when the mere business of surviving makes it hard to have the time or energy to be creative. Maybe you have a sick child, trouble in the wider family or are dealing with some other major life drama. You will need every ounce of energy just to do the essentials. I had to stop my sporadic work on this book for several weeks while I got through the nausea and tiredness of the early months of my sixth pregnancy. I had to stop again when builders came to knock our kitchen wall down and everything was chaotic. But when life calms down again after a crisis, make the most of your God-given talents and interests, not just to keep yourself sane, but for the benefit of those around you.

Mum Diary: July 2014

Overwhelmed

A mother sits on the sofa feeding her newborn. Meanwhile her three-year-old makes a puddle in the bathroom, having not quite mastered the art of undoing trousers by himself. Her four-year-old is emptying a years' worth of school work from a bag, all over the toy-strewn living room, and her six-year-old is outside making 'soup' using muddy paddling pool water and bits of mint. There is washing on the line and more in the machine, and the patio is decorated with puddles of water, half disintegrated pieces of chalk and various damp items of discarded clothing. The kitchen features the wreckage of the last meal, including sticky green puddles of melted ice lollies, which travel from the table, down chair legs and onto the floor. That was my evening. Do I laugh or cry?!

How to cope when you feel overwhelmed

The diary extract on this page is something I wrote shortly after our fourth child was born.

There are many days when I feel overwhelmed and panicked by all the tasks I must do, particularly when having to balance newborn feeds and naps with the schedules and needs of older children. My first taste of this was probably when I sat feeding my second daughter and protesting helplessly while my two-year-old smeared Vaseline on the wall. Feeling overwhelmed is one of the biggest mental challenges we face as mothers.

Chances are you don't have a plethora of servants waiting to help you (although if you can afford to get some paid help, by all means do so!). Domestic chores are piling up, there is paperwork to sort out, appointments to be made, things to be bought, emails to reply to, things that need mending, food to prepare, children who need to be taken here and there, and little ones moaning around your legs. Where to begin?! Here are some steps to follow when you feel like this:

1. Write everything down
2. Calm your insides
3. Calm your outsides
4. Plan and prepare
5. Remember that consistently doesn't have to mean daily
6. Live one day at a time
7. Don't forget your high calling and the value of your work as a mother
8. Live in grace.

Let's look at these eight steps in more detail:

1. *Write everything down.* Get it all out of your head and onto paper. Trying to hold lists inside your mind is never a good idea. I know that I forget things unless I write them down. Write down every task that is contributing to your general feeling of being overwhelmed. Keep a piece of paper and a pen next to your bed so that you are not kept awake at night mulling over the things you need to do or to remember. Write down appointments as soon as you make them, in a diary, on a wall calendar or on your phone planner.

2. *Calm your insides.* Commit everything to the Lord. Literally lay out the paper or your diary before him and tell him how you feel. 'From the end of the earth I will cry to You, when my heart is overwhelmed; Lead me to the rock that is higher than I' (Psalm 61:2 NKJV). Ask him to show you what is most important, what can be left for later and what could be delegated to someone else. I find that the more children I have, the more I must make hundreds of little daily decisions about priorities (which screaming child needs me most urgently?!). Some things really won't matter in the long run. Have you taken on certain tasks in this season of life which should probably be set aside for another time? Ask yourself which items on the list have eternal significance. Your children might always remember if you miss their school play, but in twenty years from now, whether the kitchen floor was clean or rather sticky underfoot probably won't trouble them at night. Ask for strength to do what must be done. Sometimes when I am really frazzled I find that it is good to escape from the house for half an hour to pray and get a more eternal perspective on things. Jesus often went up on a mountainside to pray away from the bustling crowds. You probably won't have time to climb a mountain, but if possible, go somewhere where you can see a bit of nature, even if that just means the local park. In these moments I empty out all my stress onto God. I am glad that he is big enough to handle it! 'Cast all your anxiety on him because he cares for you' (1 Peter 5:7 NIV). Or as Paul wrote to the Philippians,

> do not be anxious about anything, but in everything by prayer and supplication with thanksgiving let your requests be made known to God. And the peace of God, which surpasses all understanding, will guard

> your hearts and your minds in Christ Jesus. (Philippians 4:6–7)

There is no better remedy for calming your insides.

3. *Calm your outsides.* I find that I can tackle other tasks a lot more easily and serenely when the house is reasonably clean and tidy. When everything is cluttered and disorderly, the mess seems to creep into my brain and make all of life feel muddled. So, when there is a lot to do I find that it is good to spend some time cleaning and tidying up first. This gives a calm base from which to tackle other tasks. It is much easier to clean and tidy up if your children are out of the house or in bed, but if they are around and it is too cold or wet to send them into the garden to play for a bit, get them to help. Make each person put their own things away. You could put on some lively music to make it fun or play a game in which each person has to find twenty things to put away (or fifty, depending on how bad your house is that day). Set a timer to see if you can make everything look nice before it goes off. Give your two-year-old a duster, and your five-year-old the hoover … if you dare. I'm not talking about perfection, but you will feel less overwhelmed by your 'to-do' list when you can see the kitchen worktops and the living room carpet.

> Mum Diary: October 2012
> **Back to nature?**
> This morning I found S (age 3) and Y (20 months) behind the sofa, breaking my aloe vera plant into little pieces and rubbing the soil into the cushions and each other's hair.

4. *Plan and prepare in advance for everything, whenever possible.* Plan a time to tackle each item on your list. Divide the big tasks between the days in the week ahead and around your other responsibilities and commitments. If I have a busy week coming up, I like to take a big sheet of paper and draw

lines to mark out the different days. I then write down all the regular activities or appointments, like swimming and music lessons, physio appointments and meetings, before considering all the items on the 'to-do' list and seeing when the most natural time would be to fit each in.

Everyone knows that little ones are experts at creating last minute emergencies: the lost shoes, the nappy explosion when you are about to leave the house, colouring their faces or the sofa in felt-tip pens when intimidating guests are about to arrive ... Some of these things simply can't be avoided. But you can make life a little less chaotic by planning and preparing in advance for little everyday affairs as well as any big events that are coming up. I usually aim to begin leaving the house fifteen to thirty minutes before we absolutely must go, taking into consideration how many things, and children, need to be put into the car. This gives us some hope of being on time, despite the missing purse and the toddler wetting herself. Get the school bags and the changing bag ready the night before so you can just grab them in the morning. Prepare for predictable events as early as possible. Buy Christmas presents in the July sales (okay, okay, I know that's ridiculously early). Make birthday party bags or the pass-the-parcel three weeks before the party. Or maybe you have people coming to stay and want to look after them well. Two weeks before they arrive, put clean towels and sheets aside, cook meals in advance and freeze them. Then no matter what the kids do to the sofa on the day they arrive, at least your guests will have a clean bed to sleep in and something good to eat. Planning and preparing like this can help reduce feelings of being overwhelmed.

One survival tip that I find useful is looking for ways to make things serve two or more purposes. Actually, I get a bit obsessive about 'killing two birds with one stone.' So, if I have to go outside to hang washing, for example, I'll feed the guinea pig at the same time, push my toddler on the swing and take peelings to the compost bin. It's all about grouping tasks together in an efficient way. You could put a cake or two in the oven if you know it will be on for a long time cooking a lasagna. Use the bathroom heater to dry clothes as well as warming the room. Sew on that button or mend that hole while watching your toddler in the bath. If you are going to get something from your bedroom, take something with you that needs to go back there. Instead of sweeping under the kitchen table after every meal, wait until there are two or three meals' worth of crumbs on the floor before sweeping them up in one go. If you need to go to the shops in one area, wait until you have several errands to run nearby. This, I hope, helps to save time, energy, money and stress.

5. *Remember that consistently doesn't have to mean daily.* An American friend of mine, a mother of five also living in France, once shared this helpful idea. I was struggling to fit certain things into our schedule. I think at the time we were talking about teaching our bilingual children, all attending French schools, to read in English at home. She reminded me that doing something regularly and consistently doesn't have to mean that you do it every day. Do I keep my children clean? Yes, clean enough to be healthy, I hope. Do I bath them all every day? No way! Do I regularly read the Bible with my children? Yes. Do we always manage to have an official time of family worship every day? No. Am I teaching my six-year-old to read in English? Yes. Do I do this every day? No. Do I try to give some individual, special time to each child? Yes. Do I manage this every day? No. And all these things are okay. Are you putting extra pressure on yourself and your children by trying to do things that are good in themselves just a bit

too often? Could you aim to do certain things twice a week instead of feeling like a failure when you don't manage to do them every day? Life is unpredictable and busy. You never know quite how a day will pan out, especially when you have small children. Even though planning is helpful, allow yourself plenty of flexibility to accept what God sends your way. Help yourself to feel less overwhelmed by being realistic in your expectations of how regularly you can do certain things.

6. *Live one day at a time.* One of our daughters was born with congenital bilateral talipes, more commonly known as clubfoot. Most of our other children have an annoying but relatively harmless tendency to walk on their toes, especially when they have bare feet. At times this has meant many trips to the hospital for my daughter's ongoing treatment and for tests and investigations into why our other children walk around like ballerinas. One Sunday I went to church feeling discouraged about all the appointments that were approaching over the next few weeks. It takes two hours to get to the specialist hospital. Our trips there often leave us physically and emotionally exhausted. I told another church member how I felt. She said kindly, 'Don't look at all the appointments coming up. Just deal with one day at a time.' It was such simple but helpful advice. Jesus said, 'do not be anxious about tomorrow, for tomorrow will be anxious for itself. Sufficient for the day is its own trouble' (Matthew 6:34). Whatever you and your children are facing right now, don't look in despair at all the difficulties looming over the next few weeks. Just ask God for strength to do what you have to do today and then simply 'do the next thing,' as the missionary and writer Elisabeth Elliot so helpfully teaches. This will keep you from feeling overwhelmed.

There are times when you will feel overwhelmed not

because of a huge 'to-do' list, but because of a sudden crisis of urgent needs. You know, when a pot is boiling over, the baby is screaming, your toddler has just tipped fish food everywhere and your older children are squabbling. In those moments, you need to think not 'one day at a time,' but 'one task at a time.' Instead of panicking over the whole mess and muddle, running away or joining the baby screaming (which is sometimes very tempting), send up a quick prayer for help and wisdom. Then do one thing at a time. Move the boiling pan off the hob, then pick up the baby, then get the toddler away from the fish food, then sort out the squabble, and then make the child who started the fight clean up the fish food.

When I left my parent's home, I took with me quite a few of the children's books that I had grown attached to over the years. One is a book for toddlers called, *The Tidy-Up Story*.[2] It starts with a child looking at the mess in his room, knowing he has to clean it up and saying, 'I can't do it. I'm too little.' Then he realises, if I don't do it, who will? He eventually says, 'Maybe I can do it! Pick up. Put away. Tidy Up. Pick up. Put away.' He does one thing at a time until his room looks lovely at the end. I often think of that funny little book when I'm overwhelmed by the mess in the house, or in crisis moments when everyone seems to need me at once. I can't do it! I'm too little! But who's going to do it? Just pick it up and put it away. Pick it up and put it away. Refuse to look at the huge number of tasks. One thing at a time and you'll get there!

> Mum Diary: January 2012
> **Saying grace?**
> Today we asked L (age 3) to give thanks for the meal and she prayed, 'Dear Lord, thank you that I'm going to grow up to be a good wife.'

2 Karen Erickson and Maureen Roffey, *The Tidy-Up Story* (Methuen Children's Books Ltd., 1985).

7. *Don't forget your high calling and the value of your work as a mother.* I recently went to a hospital appointment and the nurse at the desk asked me about my current profession. I answered, 'mother and homemaker' in French and cringed inwardly as she wrote down, *'sans métier'* (without a profession). I thought of an elderly French friend who raised five children and often says 'Mothers are not *sans metier.* They actually have *cent métiers'* (one hundred jobs—the two phrases sound the same in French). The French term *sans activité* (without activity), which I have frequently had to tick on stress-inducing forms, is even worse. The irony! How I sometimes long for just one hour 'without activity'! I feel blessed to have such a varied schedule. As well as aiding my husband and church through work involving editing, translating, Sunday school teaching and music, on any given day my mummy tasks could comprise being a teacher, cook, cleaner, counsellor, budget manager, hairdresser, gardener, taxi driver, nurse, special-events organiser, costume designer, painter and decorator, and more besides. Your list of mummy/wife jobs will look different to mine. Maybe, like me, you dread the question, 'Do you work?' If I'm in a cheeky mood, I may well reply, 'Yes, I just don't get paid.' More often than not I'll answer, 'No, I have enough work to do at home at the moment.' I can't bring myself to say a simple 'No.' This is partly because, in my pride, I can't bear to be thought of as someone who sits around all day painting her toenails, and partly because it just wouldn't be true, even though I know what the well-meaning person is really asking.

Whether or not you also have paid employment, the fact is that if you are a mother, there are days when you work non-stop from about 6am to 11pm and sometimes during the night too. Our society sadly undervalues those who care for children, the elderly and the disabled and we are all the worse off for it. At the same time, however, the rush for cards and gifts for Mother's Day, aside from commercial motivations, shows us that most people do, deep down, appreciate their mother and value the role she played in their lives. It is dangerous to draw our sense of self-worth from what other people think about us. Only God's opinion really matters, and he has a great deal to say about the value of a mother's work. Remember those words in Proverbs:

> Her children arise and call her blessed;
>   her husband also, and he praises her:
> 'Many women do noble things,
>   but you surpass them all.' (Proverbs 31:28–29, NIV)

You are doing a noble work. I am always amazed when I read the passage in 1 Timothy about which sort of widows were worthy to receive financial support from the church:

> Let a widow be enrolled if she is not less than sixty years of age, having been the wife of one husband, and having a reputation for good works: if she has brought up children, has shown hospitality, has washed the feet of the saints, has cared for the afflicted, and has devoted herself to every good work. (1 Timothy 5:9–10)

Look at what comes first on the list of 'good works.' Taking the Gospel to unreached peoples on the other side of the world? No. Campaigning for human rights? No. The answer is bringing up children. Yes, in God's eyes, you are doing very important work. Your work as a mother, the work you do at home and the menial tasks you do to serve

> ✎ Mum Diary: December 2014
> **Whoops!**
> Today I made L (age 7) cry, by bursting out laughing when she told me that she had named her new toy pony, 'Wind.'

others, are highly valuable and can have more impact for good in the world than you might ever realise. Remember Jesus' words,

> and whoever would be first among you must be your slave, even as the Son of Man came not to be served but to serve, and to give his life as a ransom for many. (Matthew 20:27–28)

Those who care for and serve others are great in the Kingdom of God. As a mother, you are shaping the next generation. You are teaching them about God and how to live in his world in so many small ways every day. So next time someone asks you if you work, answer with confidence, 'Yes, I have a very important job. I am a mother.' And next time you feel overwhelmed, remember what a valuable role you have and how much God cares about it.

8. *Live in grace.* As Christians, we know that we cannot save our souls from hell through our own efforts. Salvation is all about God taking the first step, reaching down in unconditional love to save sinful human beings. Jesus lived a perfect life, then died on the cross, taking the blame and the punishment for the wrong things we have done. When God looks at those who trust in Jesus, he no longer sees our sin, which has been forgiven and paid for. Instead, he sees Jesus' perfect life. We began our Christian lives full of thankfulness that we don't have to earn God's favour. It is a free gift of grace. However, we sometimes forget that we must continue walking and living in that grace, every day. We do not suddenly become perfect, nor does God suddenly transform us into super-humans. But he is working in us day-by-day to make us more like Christ. We can rest in his love, even when we feel like overwhelmed failures.

While writing this book I have sometimes felt like a hypocrite. The Lord knows how often I have failed to live up to the very advice that I am seeking to give. Many of the things I mention have been learnt the hard way, through my mistakes. Living in grace means admitting our weaknesses, recognising and learning from our errors, asking for forgiveness when we fail the Lord, our husbands or our children, then moving on, resting in God's love. We do not have to try to earn his favour by being perfect mothers. 'He knows our frame; he remembers that we are dust' (Psalm 103:14). Yes, do your best, but not in a desperate, driven way, as if God will be angry with you if you don't keep to your self-imposed schedule. He knows your heart's desire to be a good mum. He sees how much you love your children. He knows how tired you are. He is bigger than your problems. He has a plan for each of your children's lives. It doesn't all depend on you. So, rest in him when you feel overwhelmed. 'Be still, and know that I am God' (Psalm 46:10).

Learning to manage our emotions at times when we feel overwhelmed by following the steps above can help us through this chapter of our lives. Don't forget to talk to someone if it all starts to feel like too much. Enjoying the good things God has given you and continuing to develop your God-given talents and interests, as you are able, will also help you to flourish mentally while you have small children.

2 Looking After Your Physical Health

Pregnancy

Motherhood really begins nine months before you hold your baby in your arms. During pregnancy you become aware of your body in a new and special way, which is why it is important to begin here as we talk about the physical side of things. What a gift to be the vehicle through whom God brings a new life into the world! It is a magical moment when you feel your baby moving inside you for the first time. In this fallen world, however, pregnancy is often accompanied by various health niggles and difficulties, some more serious than others. I admire those of you who have battled on through hyperemesis gravidarum (severe pregnancy sickness), gestational diabetes or other complications. My troubles have been limited to morning sickness, heartburn, varicose veins and low blood pressure.

As I mentioned in the introduction, this book aims to share what I have learnt through personal experience. There are many physical aspects of pregnancy and the postnatal period that are therefore not covered. Bodies are complicated, amazing creations and each woman will face different issues in her journey to becoming a mother. That is why it is so important to be cared for throughout your pregnancy by qualified midwives or doctors. In the resources section you will find a list of useful websites where you can find helpful advice about the physical side of pregnancy and childbirth. I am not a medical doctor by any means, but fortunately one of my best friends is. She has kindly read through this book to check that I have not said anything dangerous! Here we will consider several common pregnancy issues and ways to make them a little more bearable.

Morning sickness

Morning sickness should of course be called all-day sickness. Mine has always been at its worst between weeks six and twelve of pregnancy, in the afternoon and early evening. It isn't much fun lying on the sofa feeling dreadful, jumping out of the car to throw up or rushing to the bathroom while attempting to cook.

When I was two months pregnant with our first child, my husband and I had a week's holiday in Alsace, eastern France, near to where he had been at university. He wanted to introduce me to many of the Christian couples who had been kind to him while he was a student. I could barely pick at the meals they prepared to welcome us. I remember looking at a plate of chicken and green beans and wondering what on earth to do. I even threw up in one lady's mixing bowl. I learnt that having an empty tummy combined with being in a car resulted in the worst nausea for me, especially on bendy mountain roads.

The two things that helped a bit in subsequent pregnancies were sleeping as much as possible and eating little and often so that my stomach was never empty, nibbling on things that I really do love to eat. In the early weeks, my children were initially formed from pink grapefruits, Double Decker chocolate bars, crisps, skittles, marmite toast and acidic fizzy drinks, but don't tell my midwife. Yes, I know you're meant to eat a healthy, balanced diet during pregnancy, but if you feel very sick in those first months, sometimes merely surviving the day takes priority and you need to eat whatever you can keep down. Take a good pregnancy vitamin supplement which includes the recommended levels of folic acid (B9) to help prevent birth defects, drink plenty of water and get back to eating healthily as soon as you can.

Heartburn

Heartburn tends to creep up on you later in pregnancy. They say it means you will have a hairy baby, but even my baldest babies gave me heartburn. It's all to do with the valves that are meant to keep the acid within your stomach getting a little flabby (like everything else) under the effects of all those pregnancy hormones. That, combined with your stomach being increasingly squashed up under your lungs, means that those stomach juices just won't stay where they are meant to be. Gaviscon is a good remedy, so is full fat natural yoghurt and sleeping almost upright on a great big pile of pillows.

Varicose veins

Varicose veins tend to get worse with each successive pregnancy, and if your mother had them, I'm sorry but you probably will too. Mine began when I was about six months pregnant with baby number two and became bothersome a little earlier in each successive pregnancy. Thigh-high support socks are wonderful things, although I don't expect to enjoy wearing them much this coming July. They encourage normal blood flow back to the heart and make your legs a lot less achy. Put them on before you get out of bed for best results. (So it's best to shower in the evening.) Other helpful solutions are brisk walking, spraying cold water on your legs at the end of your shower if you can bear it, and of course, sitting with your feet up whenever possible. I know, if you already have children, this is almost never possible. But there are some jobs that can be done sitting down; ironing, preparing vegetables, helping with homework and so on. Get into the habit of putting your legs up while doing those things. Sit on the floor while you read to your toddler or fold washing. Walking slowly along the road at the pace of a small child can be torture. The good news is that varicose veins often virtually disappear within a couple of months of giving birth.

Blood pressure

In the second half of pregnancy I often struggle with low blood pressure in the mornings. My heart beats fast, I feel dizzy, sick, sweaty and faint. This is normally at its worst just after breakfast, when more blood is diverted from the head to the digestive system. I find that there are two seemingly opposing solutions to this: lying down until the dizzy spell passes or doing some vigorous activity to get the blood pumping around the body! A glass of cold water and some fresh air also help. It is important to have your blood pressure checked regularly throughout pregnancy. High blood pressure can be a genuine cause for concern. Along with protein in your urine, it can be a warning sign of a dangerous condition called pre-eclampsia, which occurs most often in first pregnancies. Other symptoms can include severe headaches, vision problems such as blurring or seeing flashing lights, pain below the ribs, sudden weight gain and swelling due to fluid retention, or nausea and vomiting.[3] Ensure you see a midwife or doctor urgently if you experience any of these problems.

Stretch marks

Stretch marks are another annoying pregnancy fact. Like varicose veins, whether you get them or not depends a lot on genetics and there is not a huge amount you can do about it. Gaining weight throughout your pregnancy progressively instead of suddenly can help to give your skin time to stretch. Avoiding excessive weight gain is also a good idea. You don't want to force your skin to stretch any more than it has to! Creams containing cocoa butter are meant to be helpful and can certainly stop your growing belly getting too dry and itchy. There are many products on the market which claim to work miracles, though there is little scientific proof to say whether they really do work or not. Staying hydrated is also important. Stretch marks on your tummy will shrink down along with everything else in the weeks and months following delivery. They will also fade from bright pinkish-purple to your normal skin tone but with a silvery tinge. Try to see them as scars of love, symbols of the honour of being a mother.

> Mum Diary: November 2014
> **Imagination**
> Y (age 3) came with me to get his baby sister up after her nap. Baby smiled at him and Y said, very seriously: 'She thinks I'm a dinosaur.'

Allow yourself to listen to your body during pregnancy. It is okay to slow down and take a nap. It is okay to put off until tomorrow what doesn't have to be done today (to turn a

3 https://www.nhs.uk/conditions/pre-eclampsia/

popular saying utterly inside out). Nine months isn't really very long in the grand scheme of things. It is helpful for your overall health to continue exercising normally during pregnancy if you can, provided that your usual exercise routine doesn't involve rugby, skiing, scuba diving or any other activity which could be perilous for your baby. Any sport that could cause a fall or a collision should be avoided. Remember that your hormones, in preparation for labour, will make your body more flexible than usual. So again, listen to your body and don't strain yourself.

After your baby is born

I have done some rather strange things shortly after giving birth. For three months after our first daughter was born, my sleep patterns were so messed up that I often had nightmares that my baby was trapped somewhere under the duvet cover. Several times I gave my poor, unsuspecting husband a big shove, thinking that he was lying on top of her. It would take a while for me to wake up, calm down and see that she was lying peacefully in her moses basket. The day after our fifth child arrived, I was lying in hospital half asleep when I became aware of the unpleasant drone of a mosquito. I was too tired to care if it bit me, but I was not going to let it get at my baby. I followed it with my eyes until it settled on the high ceiling. Despite my stitches, I grabbed my damp towel and climbed on a chair to whack the nasty beasty. It took several attempts, moving the chair around and getting on and off it in my nightie, during which time I really hoped that no one would come into the room.

Childbirth wounds

It can be amazing to have the help of your own mum, or another trusted older woman, in those early days as a new mother. One tip my mum gave me was to dissolve a large handful of salt in a mixing bowl of cold water, and splash this on my episiotomy wound, squatting in the shower, every couple of hours, before patting the area dry and going to lie down on my back with my knees bent. It was so soothing and helped to speed up healing.

The thought of going to the toilet can be rather terrifying after giving birth, particularly if you have had stitches. It is helpful to take one of those water bottles with a squeezable mouth-piece to hospital with you. Use it to squirt luke-warm water over yourself as you go, to dilute the urine so that it doesn't sting. Try to drink plenty of water and eat a lot of fruit and vegetables in the early days after giving birth so that you won't get constipated and have to push on your stitches. It can help to support your stitches with your hand and a pad or wad of tissue while going to the toilet. If it's any encouragement, even after my worst childbirth wounds, the reality of using the bathroom wasn't as bad as I had feared!

Doing pelvic floor exercises throughout pregnancy, and especially after labour, increases blood flow to the area and can help to speed up healing. Your pelvic floor muscles are the ones you use to control when you go to the toilet. They are crucial for supporting many organs yet suffer a lot of strain during pregnancy and childbirth. Weakness can lead to incontinence and other problems. It is a good idea to ask your midwife for advice about how to tone up these muscles after giving birth, to avoid complications later in life.

After-pains

After-pains are the tummy cramps you may experience after giving birth as your uterus begins to contract. These often feel like period pain and can be awful in the first few days after the delivery, particularly while breastfeeding. When your baby feeds, your body releases oxytocin, making the muscles contract. This is a good thing because it prevents excessive bleeding and makes your tummy shrink, but the pains tend to be worse the more babies you have had. After my fifth child they were so bad that I threw up when breastfeeding (not on the baby, thankfully). When baby number six arrived, I made sure I took paracetamol and ibuprofen regularly (the maximum safe dose!) beginning as soon as possible after childbirth. I didn't feel the after-pains at all which was a great relief. Ibuprofen is considered safe to use for a limited time during breastfeeding, though should be avoided in pregnancy. Consult your doctor or midwife if you are not sure which medicines are safe for your personal needs. A hot water bottle can also be helpful.

Feeding yourself

It is a strange phenomenon that newborns nearly always wake up and cry just when someone brings your dinner in. Maybe they smell the food and want some too. Don't feel guilty about letting your baby grizzle for a few minutes while you eat your dinner, especially if you are breastfeeding. You need to eat well to make milk! Childbirth leaves you starving hungry. The egg and ham salad they brought along after my first delivery is forever etched in my mind as the most amazing meal I have ever tasted. Several hours later I ate a whole packet of Maltesers in one go at 3am. I lost quite a lot of blood giving birth to number four, which left me weak and shaky. Nevertheless, I was determined to break open the rather hard roll they brought in on a tray at 2am, just after my husband had gone home, even though I could barely hold the knife. I *had* to get the roll open to put the butter and jam on. I mean, I needed those calories and didn't fancy eating the butter by itself. The midwife had also forgotten to put a spoon on the tray, so I slurped the yoghurt out of the pot and scooped up the last bit with my fingers.

The French medical system is wonderful. You are given your own en-suite room on the postnatal ward and they look after you for four days. Nevertheless, they don't bring new mothers enough breakfast. One small roll with butter and jam and one hot drink doesn't seem much when you have been up all night with a new baby. But why am I talking about this? Basically, to tell you to take extra food with you to hospital. Fill the gaps in your suitcase with good things to keep you nourished. And say 'yes' when they ask if you'd like a hot drink, even if you don't actually want it. Your husband will appreciate it.

> ✎ Mum Diary: March 2012
> **Compliments**
> L (age 4): 'This pie is essscelent. You're a very pretty cooker Mummy.' (What a shame it came out of a packet!)

Cooking has always felt impossible to me during the first few months after having a baby. My husband is very good at many things, but he would be the first to admit that cooking is not one of them. So, after I have used up the meals that I put in the freezer before the baby came along, and the things that my mum added afterwards, I feel a little bit lost. Babies demand so much time.

In the last few years our church has started a ministry of recruiting people on a rota to take one hot meal per day to families that have a new baby, for a week or two after mother and baby leave hospital. If your church does not yet do this, could you be the first to suggest it for the next lady who is expecting? Having a rota means that it is not too much of a burden for any one person, but this can make a huge difference to the family you are serving.

Once you do have to cope alone, it is a good idea to start cooking your main meal as early as possible during the day. One-pot casseroles that you can throw into a slow cooker to simmer for hours are wonderful. But whatever you are making, if you start early on you have a good chance of having something nice to eat in the evening, even if you are interrupted twenty times whilst cooking it. Keep a good supply of easy food on hand too. Fish fingers, frozen vegetables, baked beans and other things in tins can sometimes save the day. Eating well is very important when you have a new baby and all your family will appreciate a good meal even if you manage to get little else done in the day. Throughout the months after giving birth, continue to take vitamins, get your iron levels checked regularly and make nutritious eating a priority.

Feeding your baby

I really struggled to position my first baby for breastfeeding and came very close to giving up. Each feed was agony until, seven long days after the birth, a midwife eventually showed me how to latch her on correctly. I know many mothers who have tried to breastfeed, struggled for all sorts of reasons, cried buckets of tears and eventually switched to formula. Please don't feel guilty if this describes you. In your adult life, has anyone ever asked you if you were breast or bottle fed (the mothers in your antenatal class don't count)? How you were fed simply becomes irrelevant later on. Of course, breastmilk is designed by God and has all sorts of health benefits for your baby, especially antibodies which can protect your baby from infections. It changes throughout the day and over time as your baby develops. Formula is made by experts to mimic breastmilk as much as possible and to meet all your baby's nutritional needs. It has come on a long way since the days when my grandma was encouraged to feed my aunty diluted evaporated milk in Singapore. Even my aunty survived. The most important thing is that your baby is fed and loved.

One reason I didn't ask for more help with breastfeeding during the first week was because I had read that you should expect it to be hard to start with. I therefore thought that what I was experiencing was normal. If you do find breastfeeding hard for whatever reason, ask to see a lactation consultant. Sometimes there may be a medical reason behind your difficulty, such as the baby having a tongue tie. Hopefully these things will be spotted quickly by professionals. Even when your baby is correctly latched on, you may have slightly sore nipples for a few weeks, particularly at the beginning of each feed, while your breasts get used to being sucked. However, the pain should not be severe and if you do have cracks and crevasses, it is likely that the baby is not latched on well. Keep asking for advice until you find someone who can help you to feed comfortably.

You can feed your baby in many different positions. While the following step-by-step guide is no substitute for having someone there who can help you to get the hang of it, here is how I was taught to latch my baby on to feed in a standard 'cross-over' or 'cross-cradle' position:

- *To feed your baby from your left breast:* Tuck his bottom into the bend of your right elbow, with your right hand supporting his head and neck loosely, so that you can tilt his head backwards.

- Make sure your baby is fully turned with his 'tummy to mummy.'
- With your other hand, make a C shape to cup round your left breast.
- At this point your baby's nose should be about level with your nipple.
- As you bring your baby close to feed, tilt his head back slightly, so that his bottom lip touches you first, just outside the areola (the darker area around your nipple).When his lower lip touches you, he should automatically open his mouth wide. If he doesn't, try again. Don't let him grab just a little bit of nipple with a half-open mouth! Wait until that mouth is open wide!
- When he opens his mouth, quickly use your left hand, still in a C shape, to guide the nipple and as much breast as possible into his mouth.
- If his lips are not totally flayed apart and folded outwards, use a finger to pull them out a bit more so that the nipple is as deep inside his mouth as possible.
- You should start to hear swallowing as the milk is let down. Clicking sounds normally mean that there is a problem with the latch.
- It is good to let the baby drain one breast completely before swapping to the other, so that he gets the richer hind-milk as well as the more watery fore-milk. Babies may not want to drink from both breasts in one feed. Start with the other breast next time.
- Your baby may come off the breast himself when he

has had enough. If not, put your finger gently into the corner of his mouth to release the suction.

- Newborns sometimes get sleepy when feeding and stop sucking. To keep them awake, try tickling their feet, taking off some of their clothes and having plenty of skin to skin contact.

It is said that rubbing a little breastmilk onto your nipples will help if they are sore, but I have found that a tiny bit of Vaseline, applied just after a feed, is more effective. The hospital in France gave me a little pot of lanolin to use, but it made me itch! If you are not allergic to lanolin, it may be worth a try. Once you and your baby get into the swing of things, breastfeeding can be a real pleasure and much more convenient than having to carry bottles around. Disposable breast pads are useful at the beginning when your milk supply is settling down and you leak a lot at random moments. They can be itchy though! Once baby and I had got into a routine, I found washable pads more comfortable and economical, though they don't offer so much protection from large leaks.

An expectant mother recently asked me about public breastfeeding. When I visited Morocco I was surprised that in a Muslim culture that generally puts so much emphasis on women's modesty, when mothers needed to breastfeed they simply unzipped the top of their floor-length djellabas and let everything hang out, quite literally! Over the last few years there has been a lot of campaigning on social media for a greater acceptance of public breastfeeding in Europe and America. These campaigns typically highlight the inconsistency of western public opinion, which sometimes frowns on mothers for breastfeeding in public, yet is quite happy with billboards advertising seductive lingerie in which the models are virtually naked. While I agree with the general aim of these campaigns—that mothers should not be criticised for feeding their babies outside the home—there is also no need to go to the opposite extreme and show your breasts to the world.

Those who argue that there is no need for modesty because breasts are simply milk machines, designed only to nurture babies, should remember that the Bible itself speaks of breasts in the context of female sexuality, almost as often as it speaks of their use in nursing babies. Think, for example, of these verses in the Song of Songs which describe the intimate relationship of married lovers: 'Your stature is like a palm tree, and your breasts are like its clusters. I say I will climb the palm tree and lay hold of its fruit. Oh may your breasts be like clusters of the vine' (Song of Songs 7:7–8). Or in Proverbs: 'Let your fountain be blessed, and rejoice in the wife of your youth, a lovely deer, a graceful doe. Let her breasts fill you at all times with delight; be intoxicated always in her love' (Proverbs 5:18–19). So breasts should not be viewed merely as milk factories. Their sexual appeal was designed by God, not imposed on them by our sleazy consumer culture. This was confirmed to me once when I sat down to feed my son in our living room about a year after our move to France—throwing caution to the wind because I thought I was alone at home—and looked up to find our middle-aged neighbour staring at me through the window from behind his garden wall, smirking and nodding in a horrid lecherous manner. I kept the shutters closed on that side of the house until our planned moving date which was fortunately just three weeks later! The thought of that incident still gives me the creeps.

On the other hand, what could be more natural and beautiful than a woman feeding her baby using the means that God himself has provided? No woman should be criticised for doing so. I remember taking all my children shopping on one extremely hot summer day. As we pulled into the car park, the baby was crying and I knew she needed a feed. I couldn't bear to sit in the boiling car, so I opened the boot and sat there in its shade to feed her. A lady with children soon walked by and looked at me as if I were a disgusting piece of scum, even though I don't believe a single bit of flesh was visible. No mother should have to face looks like that or disparaging comments, for meeting her baby's needs.

So, what is the solution? As with many things, the middle ground is often the most sensible way to proceed. There are ways to breastfeed discreetly without resorting to the unpleasant business of hiding in a public toilet or burying your baby under suffocating sheets. When you first start to breastfeed, latching the baby on can be a bit tricky and not easy to do discreetly. However, once you get used to doing this, it is quite possible to feed your baby in public without showing any unnecessary flesh.

- Try to wear two-part outfits whenever possible (top and trousers or skirt) rather than dresses. I once wore a one-piece dress with a zip at the back to a wedding while I was still breastfeeding. On that occasion I really had no choice but to hide in the toilets to feed, since I had to take the whole dress off to do so!
- Wear a nursing bra that has clips near the shoulders. You can unclip one side and fold it down inside your clothes, by putting your hand through the neck of your top.
- Bump bands are very useful throughout pregnancy and breastfeeding. They are elasticated bands of material, like the bottom half of a t-shirt. In pregnancy, before

you are big enough to need maternity clothes, you can fasten your jeans loosely with an elastic band looped through the button hole and over the button. The bump band goes on top to hide the unfastened zip. It also bridges the gap between your top and trousers, which gets bigger as your bump grows and can help you not to have to move into maternity clothes so early. Throughout breastfeeding you can use bump bands so that your tummy doesn't have to be bared to all as you lift your top to feed. If you have already folded your nursing bra down, very little skin will show.

- If you don't have any bump bands, a strappy vest top (preferably an old one with saggy straps!) worn under your clothes, can serve the same purpose. Before a feed, just pull the top down so that the neckline that normally sits above the bust is now below it.
- Wearing an open cardigan or light jacket can also be practical for keeping everything hidden from the side while latching your baby on. You can then adjust your clothes and it will look like you are just holding your baby. I remember feeding one of my daughters at the back of church when an old man approached me to admire her, thinking she was asleep. I don't think he realised before or afterwards that I was breastfeeding!
- For more ideas on which clothes work well for breastfeeding, see the Facebook page 'Can I breastfeed in it?'

If a bit of flesh does show, it's really not a big deal. Remember that what you are doing is normal and natural. You are not trying to seduce anyone, and no one in their right mind will imagine that you are. Breastfeeding discreetly in public can get trickier when your baby is a bit older and wants to turn her head to look for the source of any slight sound. At this stage it is generally easier to find a secluded room to breastfeed in if you have that option. In the UK there are quite a few shops, especially Mothercare, Boots, Ikea and other shops selling baby equipment, that have practical rooms where you can go to feed and change a baby. If possible, find out about these before your little one arrives.

Rest

Don't feel guilty about having afternoon naps, or morning naps for that matter. God made us to need sleep and chances are your baby won't let you have much of it at night, so try to catch up a bit another time. Today's world moves at such a fast pace. Electricity can give us 24-hour light, and 24-hour work if we want. We can become driven by an unhealthy need to perform, to do more, to stay up to date with everything and everyone. But that is not how God wants us to live. Right from the beginning of time he made the night for sleeping and a rest day once a week. 'It is in vain that you rise up early and go late to rest, eating the bread of anxious toil; for he gives to his beloved sleep' (Psalm 127:2). Taking time to catch up on missed sleep is not a sign of laziness. (Although spending all your time in bed can be, of course. I'm not telling you to sleep your life away.) It demonstrates a quiet trust in God that your world will not fall to pieces while you are asleep. Sleep whenever you can in those early months of motherhood.

> Mum Diary: May 2017
> **Bank holidays**
> Most people would think of having a lie-in on a bank holiday. Not my kids. They were up bright and early so that they could rush outside and paint the walls of the house with water.

It is also a good idea to give yourself a day off from time to time. The duties of motherhood are relentless. It is not like being an employee and knowing that you have a certain amount of holiday to take each year. If you don't take the initiative to organise some time away from it all occasionally, no one will do it for you. Jesus once saw that his disciples were exhausted. So many people were clamouring after them that they did not even have a chance to eat. Jesus said to them, 'Come with me by yourselves to a quiet place and get some rest' (Mark 6:31 NIV). We can sometimes feel like those disciples, surrounded all day and night by little people with needs. How can we put Jesus' words into practice and be refreshed?

- *'Come with me.'* Why not ask your husband or a friend if they could take over your normal responsibilities for a few hours so that you can go out and have a change of scene? Whatever we do to escape, we need to do it with Jesus. Getting away from it all for a time doesn't give us licence to let down our guard, watch inappropriate films or go to places we know are not pleasing to God. We need to imagine taking Jesus with us. He promised to give rest to those who are weary and burdened (Matthew 11:28). Spending some time with Jesus during your break, by reading his Word, praying and praising him, will refresh your soul. Remember, 'they who wait for the Lord shall renew their strength; they shall mount up with wings like eagles; they shall run and not be weary; they shall walk and not faint' (Isaiah 40:31).

- *'By yourselves.'* Alone time is bliss to a busy mother. It can give us new perspective on our role and more energy and motivation to return to it wholeheartedly.

- *'To a quiet place.'* Quietness is another thing that

mothers crave! You could try going for a walk by a river with a good book and a picnic, but sometimes what you need is a chance to do certain activities that are difficult with noisy children around. Perhaps having your hair cut, eating in a restaurant, going to the cinema or shopping with a friend are relaxing for you.

- *'Get some rest.'* Whatever you do for a break, keep this aim in sight and don't dash around madly trying to get a million things done before you return home.

It is interesting that on the particular occasion recorded in the Gospel of Matthew, Jesus and his disciples didn't actually get much chance to rest, except while they were on the boat. A whole load of people had seen where they were heading and ran around the lake to get to the solitary place before them. Jesus had started out with concern that the disciples didn't have a chance to eat. He ended up, out of his great compassion, teaching and feeding the five thousand! Sometimes despite our best efforts to have some time away from it all, something happens to interrupt our plans. Our child (or the babysitter) is ill, or our husband has to go into work unexpectedly. We need grace to see those interruptions as opportunities, trusting that God will give us strength and there will be other more appropriate times to rest.

Perhaps our definition of rest is sometimes too narrow. Being a bit of an introvert, I tend to define rest as alone time. Of all my responsibilities, caring for my children involves the most hard work, so it is easy to start seeing time without them around as the epitome of rest (every mother has days when her children's bedtime can't come soon enough). But rest can be a state of mind or soul as much as a physical reality. David wrote, 'Truly my soul finds rest in God' (Psalm 62:1 NIV). A heart that quietly trusts God in every circumstance is a heart at rest. I don't want to view my children simply as creators of hard work, so I have asked God to help me learn to rest even when I am with my little ones, both through having a soul at rest in God and through finding activities that we can all enjoy together. I did recently go on a shopping trip with my two older girls that, to my surprise, felt like a pleasure and not a trial. It showed me that as the children get older, resting in their company will hopefully get easier.

Exercise

Get some exercise outdoors whenever possible. Being a mother is very physical. You are forever squatting to pick up toys and toddlers, shaking duvets into duvet covers, lugging piles of washing or shopping around and racing up to school a little bit late. I have found that I have a lot more energy and cope better with daily tasks, since starting to attend a local fitness class. I often have to drag myself there reluctantly but come home feeling much more alive. I don't think I would be very motivated to exercise on my own, so having a class to attend is helpful. The woman of Proverbs 31 was strong as well as wise: 'She dresses herself with strength and makes her arms strong' (Proverbs 31:17). Exercise not only helps you physically, it is also very important for your mental and emotional wellbeing. Sometimes when I feel a bit down, I can trace it directly back to not having exercised as much as normal.

Hand care

'The hands that rock the cradle rule the world,' goes the well-known saying. Unfortunately, those hands may also be constantly dry and sore. Protect your mummy-hands—which are always in water. Be strict with yourself about wearing gloves—warm ones to protect you from the cold wind (especially when pushing a pushchair), solid ones for gardening and big projects, rubber ones for housework and cheap disposable ones for cleaning the pet cage or doing messy cooking. I have found that taking cod liver oil helps to protect skin from the inside out, but it is not recommended during pregnancy due to its high vitamin A content. Put hand cream in all your bags, by all your sinks, in the car, in the pushchair and by your bed! (It's a good idea to put tissues and baby wipes all over the place too.) Dry skin is more vulnerable to allergic reactions. If your hands become itchy as well as dry, see your doctor as you may need a special cream.

Taking care of your appearance

It is important to continue taking care of your appearance when you are a mother. During the first few weeks with a newborn, simply having a shower can seem impossible, but it does get easier! If you are a Christian, you know that your body is the temple of the Holy Spirit. You are made in the image of God. You are a daughter of the King of Kings and you are unique and beautiful, yes, even with stretch marks, bags under your eyes and the extra weight you gained in pregnancy. You honour God by looking after your body. Your husband wants to see you making an effort to look nice and it will do a lot for your own sense of wellbeing and dignity.

> Mum Diary: May 2017
> **Another compliment?**
> Y (age 6): 'Mummy, how old are you?'
> Mum: 'I'm 32'
> Y: 'But you're not that big. 32 means you should be up to the roof of the house!'

Of course, there are some days when your work at home means you can serve your family better wearing tracksuit bottoms and old t-shirts. There is nothing I enjoy more than putting on my old paint-stained jeans and faded university Christian Union hoody to tackle a messy project. But don't let that become your permanent look! Get your hair cut in a way that suits you and wear a little make-up if you are into that. Just a bit of lipstick, in the colour that your cheeks go when you pinch them, can brighten your whole face. Look out for clothes for yourself in the sales, not just for your children. If you are not sure what would look nice on you, particularly if having babies has changed the shape of your body, ask a friend who dresses tastefully for some help.

After giving birth, you suddenly feel light and slim, even though your tummy looks like a cross between a half-deflated balloon and a jelly blancmange. Being able to breathe properly again is probably a big part of this. This sensation of lightness soon wears off, however, when you get home and find that you have no hope of squeezing into even your 'fat jeans.' There is no question that motherhood changes your body in many ways. It took nine months to gain those pregnancy pounds and your body needs reserves to get through the gruelling first months of sleepless nights and breastfeeding. Don't let the media's unrealistic idea of female beauty make you miserable. Enjoy being curvy! You are female! You have given birth to a precious new human being! If you eat sensibly and exercise safely, the weight will gradually drop off, though this takes longer for some people than others.

Looking after your physical health in these ways not only glorifies God, your Creator, but will also give you more energy to tackle all the demands of motherhood with joy and optimism.

3 Looking After Your Spiritual Health

What you believe about God and how well you know him will have a direct impact on how you cope with life's challenges, and not just those related to motherhood. This is why it is so important to look after your soul even, and especially, during the busiest periods.

Cultivate your relationship with God

Trusting in God's sovereignty and eternal love will keep you calm when you are worried about one of your children. Knowing that he will reward your work will help you to persevere when you are tired of serving others. Believing that there is 'no condemnation for those who are in Christ Jesus' (Romans 8:1) will help you to repent and move on when you know that you have failed as a mother. We need to speak these truths to ourselves when our feelings are telling us otherwise. The

> Mum Diary: July 2012
> **Literal interpretation**
> After a family worship time on Proverbs and being careful how we speak and use our tongues, S (age 2½) prayed: 'Dear Lord, thank you for a nice day. Help us not to keep sticking our tongues out.'

Psalmist does this in Psalm 42: 'Why are you cast down, O my soul, and why are you in turmoil within me? Hope in God; for I shall again praise him, my salvation' (Psalm 42:5). He talks to himself, reminding himself of God's goodness and focusing on that instead of on how he feels. To be able to do this, we need to have God's Word in our hearts. How can we cultivate our relationship with God as mothers?

Your 'quiet time' doesn't have to be quiet, although if you can set aside some quiet moments with God, great! Ideally it is wise to spend time talking to God each morning to prepare your heart for the day ahead before you interact with anyone else, but for mothers this can be a real challenge. I have sometimes tried to get up before the children in order to read my Bible, but our children seem to have super-sensitive hearing that makes them pop awake as soon as my feet touch the floor. I even bought a vibrating under-pillow alarm clock, hoping that they wouldn't hear it, but their mummy sensor still detected movement and bang went all hope of an alone time. There is no point getting the whole house up at the crack of dawn. I felt guilty about this in the past, but I have learnt to believe that God understands our situations even better than we do ourselves. After all, 'his understanding is unsearchable' (Isaiah 40:28). The Lord knows when you are exhausted and too tired to read or pray, from being up all night with a newborn or a sick child. He also knows when you miss your quiet time because you spent too long watching films the night before instead!

One mother told me that the phrase 'flexible discipline' has been helpful to her. You need to be disciplined in finding time to feed your soul, but you don't have to have a rigid routine. What works for you will change in each season of life. Maybe things will be different when I have a house full of teenagers who don't want to get up in the morning. Right now, the best time for me to read God's Word is when our four oldest children have been deposited at school and I can sit down with a quiet cuppa while my twenty-month-old toddles around. When breastfeeding, I find it good to try to read the Bible during the baby's first feed of the day, if I am awake enough to concentrate, before I allow myself to read other things. I love the verse, 'He will tend his flock like a shepherd; he will gather the lambs in his arms; he will carry them in his bosom, and gently lead those that are with young' (Isaiah 40:11). It is God who made you a mother and he knows the limitations that this season brings. Jesus showed this compassion for mothers when he spoke prophetically about difficult times in the last days; 'alas for women who are pregnant and for those who are nursing infants' (Matthew 24:19). Our relationship with God should be just that, a *relationship* with our heavenly Father, not a strict, formal, guilt-driven routine.

God wants us to be in fellowship with him throughout the day. We are told to 'pray without ceasing' (1 Thessalonians 5:17). Talk to God while you are washing dishes, driving to pick up the kids or cutting the grass. Pray with your toddler on your knee. He is with you even in the chaos of family life. Meeting to pray with other mothers or an older lady can also be helpful. I have attended many ladies' prayer meetings at which my toddlers played on the floor with other little ones in the centre of the group, while the grown-ups talked and prayed.

> Mum Diary: September 2015
> **Omniscience**
> Y (age 4): 'Can Jesus see inside our tummies?'

Following a simple Bible reading plan can keep you spiritually fed with some structure even if you never read at the same time each day and are three months behind. Hearing from God is what matters, even if you only read a little at a time. If you want to read while feeding your baby, it is useful to have God's Word on an electronic device so that you don't need to hold a book open. I have found it helpful to have the 'One-Year Bible' on my Kindle. The next section to read is always right there, with a passage for each day from the Old Testament, New Testament, Psalms and Proverbs. I rarely read all four sections at once, but I like the fact that I never lose my place (except when my toddler has found it first and clicked a few pages ahead). And since my Kindle has a bright pink cover, I don't lose it as often as my Bible either! There are many great Bible apps for phones. These permit you to read easily while your children are having their swimming lessons or if you arrive at the school gate a few minutes early. Listen to Christian radio programmes or sermons on the Internet while doing chores. I highly recommend 'Revive Our Hearts,'[4] a ministry for women started by Elisabeth Elliott (known originally as 'Gateway to Joy') and now featuring faithful and relevant Bible teaching by Nancy DeMoss Wolgemuth.

Singing Christian songs and hymns while you work around the home can also help you to stay in communion with God, reminding you of the truths that keep you grounded and lifting your vision from the mundane to the eternal. Pin up the words of a favourite or helpful hymn by the kitchen sink so that you can memorise it slowly. Go to church, even if you are always late and spend most of your time in the creche. It will do you good to be with other believers and your children will see that it is important to you and will learn to love your church family.

---

4 www.reviveourhearts.com

Unload your guilt

We have already discussed the need to live in grace by embracing God's forgiveness when we fail as mothers. Sometimes we feel guilty because we really have done something wrong, like losing our temper and screaming at our children, or breaking the speed limit because we didn't want to get a reputation for always being late. In these situations, a guilty conscience, or 'conviction of sin' as it's often termed, is a good thing if it makes us run to Christ. Talking to other Christian mothers, however, I have realised that many of us carry around a vague sense of condemnation *most of the time*, often for reasons that look ridiculous once we consider them rationally.

Our family recently went to a retreat for pastors and their wives and children. As I thanked the people who ran the children's programme at the end of the week, I nearly cried as they said, 'Your children are lovely. You're doing a great job. Keep up the good work.' I realised that most of the time I don't feel at all as if I am doing a great job. Quite the opposite. I tend to think that since I am finding motherhood hard, I must be doing something wrong. I am forgetful of grace. I was touched to hear other people say that they thought I was doing something right!

Can you relate to any of the following guilt trips? Guilty because I can't afford to let my daughter have horse riding lessons. Guilty because I had to increase the food budget by fifty percent compared to a few years ago when our family was smaller. Guilty for being late to a meeting, even though it was because the baby threw up on me. Guilty for watching a film while the children had their nap. Guilty because I bought myself new shoes, even though my old ones were falling apart. Guilty for not feeding the children home-cooked food today, even though I was out most of the time, taking them to appointments. Guilty when the children all seem grumpy and upset, because surely if I was a better mother, they would always be happy, right? Guilty when the house is in a mess because I made the children's needs a priority. Guilty when the house is tidy, because I sat my children in front of a DVD for two hours in order to achieve it. Guilty because my toddler wasn't potty trained as early as her siblings. Guilty for asking for help, because in this age of contraception, I chose to have these babies, and won't people think that I should just accept the consequences and manage alone? (What if people start seeing me like 'the old woman who lived in a shoe, who had so many children she didn't know what to do'?) Guilty because I don't do all those things that another mother does. Guilty, guilty, guilty! Maybe you didn't really want to read this book because you were afraid it might make you feel even more guilty.

In one sense, it is good to have a humble opinion of ourselves. The Bible says, 'Clothe yourselves, all of you, with humility toward one another, for "God opposes the proud but gives grace to the humble." Humble yourselves, therefore, under the mighty hand of God so that at the proper time he may exalt you' (1 Peter 5:5–6). The book of Proverbs lists 'haughty eyes' among seven things that the Lord hates (Proverbs 6:16–19). Our culture tells us to walk in pride, to have confidence in ourselves. This is clearly not the answer. So what is? How do we avoid both a prideful, worldly attitude, and walking around under a cloud of condemnation? The answer is to find our identity in Christ. When tempted to be proud we need to remember the price Jesus had to pay to take away our sin. Even our best actions are tainted with sin, like filthy rags (Isaiah 64:6). When feeling condemned, we must remember that God loves us with an everlasting love (Jeremiah 31:3), that our sins have been removed as far as the east is from the west (Psalm 103:12), that as we find our identity in Christ who lived a perfect life on our behalf, we are considered by God to be pure and free.

It is helpful to ask yourself a few questions to determine whether your guilt is justified: Have I really done something wrong? If so, I need to repent and ask God for forgiveness. If not, what is the underlying reason for my feeling of condemnation? Sometimes you will realise that you are just being silly! Often, you will identify lies that you have believed, worldly thought patterns or even idols that are feeding your thoughts. Then ask yourself which Scriptures you could use to help yourself think biblically about the subject. Perhaps you could grab a piece of paper and make a table like the one below. Write down all the things you feel a vague sense of guilt over as a mother, then analyse what is driving those thoughts and how you can fight them with the truth. Finally, pray that the truth will penetrate your heart and influence your feelings.

Reason for guilt	**Have I really done something wrong?**	**What wrong thoughts/ lies/ idols are feeding my sin or unjustified sense of condemnation?**	**What does the Bible say that could help me correct my thoughts?**
Speeding to get to church on time	Yes	Fear of what people will think of me if I am late again. The idol of reputation.	Obey those in authority (Titus 3:1). Do what is right, even when no one else can see you, because we should live to please God, not people (Ephesians 6:6).
Increasing the food budget	No	Making an idol out of being frugal instead of accepting that our family is now bigger and food prices have increased. Fear of not being able to afford other things we need—lack of trust in God's provision.	We must provide for our families (1 Timothy 5:8). God has promised to give us all we need (Matthew 6:25–34).

The children are all grumpy today so I must be a bad mother	No	Wanting to feel in control. The lie that if I was a good mother my children would always be happy.	We live in a fallen world. If my children are poorly or sad, it isn't necessarily my fault (John 16:33). They also have sinful natures (Romans 3:23, Psalm 51:5). Moaning and complaining, manipulation and selfishness are all playing a role here.
Guilty for asking for help	No	Pride—thinking I can manage alone or fear of letting others see my weakness. Doubting motives or not wanting to burden others.	We need other people! We are meant to encourage one another (1 Thessalonians 5:11) and use our gifts to serve each other (Galatians 5:13). People at church love us and are glad to have a chance to help. They are not judging me for having too many children! Even in this age of contraception, God is in ultimate control of my fertility and he gave me these little ones.
Guilty for not doing the things that another mother does	No	My ego—wanting to be better than or as good as others. Am I unwilling to learn from others?	We all have different gifts (Romans 12:3–8). We are all uniquely created (Psalm 139:14). She has her burdens and struggles too, that I may know nothing about. Comparing ourselves to others is not wise (2 Corinthians 10:12).

When we look at the underlying causes of our guilty feelings, we often find that the things we need to repent of are not the surface reasons we give for feeling guilty, but the pride, idols or wrong thoughts that are behind them. Remember, too, that the fact that you are struggling does not necessarily mean that you are doing it all wrong. We have many limitations and live in a fallen world where Jesus said we 'will have tribulation' (John 16:33). Think about all the godly people in the Bible

> Mum Diary: May 2013
> **Burdens**
> L, looking at a 'Pilgrim's Progress' cartoon: 'What's that big bag on the man's back?'
> Mum: 'It's a burden, a heavy bag that's a picture of his sin. When he trusts in Jesus, the burden falls off.'
> S (age 3½): 'Does his bag have a bird in?'

who struggled, even though they were doing just what God wanted them to do: Joseph, Daniel, Moses, Jeremiah, Elijah, Jesus himself. Satan is often referred to in Scripture as 'the Accuser.' I expect he loves it when Christian mothers feel weighed down by guilt. Remember that there is 'now no condemnation for those who are in Christ Jesus' (Romans 8:1). No condemnation! We can put away false guilt about things that are outside our control. Thanks to the cross of Christ, we can also banish the burden of genuine guilt. Jesus has carried it for us. We are free!

Be thankful for opportunities to grow more Christlike

Here are four areas in which motherhood will give you opportunities to grow in grace:

Motherhood teaches us how to make sacrifices for the good of others

As we set aside our own preferences in order to love and serve our children, we are giving them a glimpse of the sacrificial love of Christ. The eternal Son of God left his glory in heaven to serve us sinners. The One who made the stars washed the disciples' grubby feet. The One who designed hundreds of varieties of trees, became a humble carpenter and was eventually nailed to a piece of wood as he bore the punishment that we deserve for our sin. If Jesus was willing to do this much for us, how much more should we be willing to lay down our own desires in order to serve others! He can help us to overcome our selfishness and minister to our families. Four verses come to mind when thinking about the concept of dying to oneself so that we can give life and love to others:

> Greater love has no one than this, that someone lay down his life for his friends. (John 15:13)

> For we who live are always being given over to death for Jesus' sake, so that the life of Jesus also may be manifested in our mortal flesh. (2 Corinthians 4:11)

> Truly, truly, I say to you, unless a grain of wheat falls into the earth and dies, it remains alone; but if it dies, it bears much fruit. (John 12:24)

> If anyone would come after me, let him deny himself and take up his cross and follow me. For whoever would save his life will lose it, but whoever loses his life for my sake will find it. (Matthew 16:24–25)

Mothers learn to 'lay down their lives' for their children in many small ways every day. Childbirth itself is an excellent picture of laying down one's life in order to give life to others (though not literally of course, since in Europe, at least, death in childbirth is now unusual). Each time a baby cries in the night and you must drag yourself out of your warm bed; each time you listen with patience to a story you've already heard ten times before; each time you clean up a mess that you had no part in making, you are demonstrating a little bit of what it means to lay down your life for others. How often we do these things reluctantly! Yet if we ask God to use everyday challenges to sanctify us and make us more like Christ, we will gradually find our attitudes changing and the love of Jesus shining through us. Never forget that this type of death is followed by resurrection. The path to glory is humility. The path to life is death. God will make something beautiful out of any sacrifice you make for him.

Motherhood teaches us patience and self-control

We would like to be able to wake up one morning and find that we have suddenly been transformed into godly, patient mothers. But God uses the fires of life to refine us. As Job said, 'when he has tried me, I shall come out as gold' (Job 23:10). Your children will push your patience to its limits and beyond. They will pour cereal and milk all over the floor and themselves when you are about to go to church. They will be silly and giggly when you are tired and have a headache. We need to humbly confess our weaknesses and ask God to use these daily challenges to make us patient. Or maybe it's the 'stupid inanimate object' that reveals your impatience? The pushchair that refuses to fit in the car boot even though it did yesterday or the freezer drawer that won't open because something has got wedged under the drawer above? Do child car seats drive you crazy with frustration? I thought so. You're not alone. Here's how it goes:

You think you are about to leave the house on time, but then you remember that the toddler's car seat is in the garage because you took it out to fit a piece of furniture in the car two days ago. You carefully manoeuvre the bulky car seat into position, trying not to bash the car door on the wall, and wish your fingers were two inches longer as you try to get the belt through the back of it in the right place. You put your toddler in and the straps are too tight because it is colder today than last time he sat in it and he is therefore wearing more clothes. So, you make the straps bigger but then realise he is sitting on the central buckle. You try not to hurt him while prising it out from between his legs. Meanwhile your hair gets caught in his jumper zip and you discover quite a lot of biscuit crumbs. Your toddler, getting cross and impatient while you are trying to untangle your hair, pushes out his chest, making it impossible to do up the buckle. You finally clip him in, jump into the driver's seat and realise you have left the car key on the floor next to your toddler. You retrieve the car key and pull out of the drive breathing a sigh of relief, at which point your six-year-old yells, 'Mummy, I can't do up my belt!' Aaaargh!

What is the solution? Do I have a survival tip for this? Sadly, no. I, for one, am looking forward to the day when someone invents self-closing child car restraints. A friend told me recently that she thinks child car seats are a sneaky form of family planning. The only positive thing I can say is that children do grow, and eventually there comes a marvellous day when they are tall enough and heavy enough to no longer need a car seat and they can buckle themselves in. However, my daily fight to remain calm and patient in the face of uncooperative child car restraints is just one example of how motherhood is a school of patience and self-control—if you allow it to be. Imagining Jesus sitting there in the car with you can help you to keep your temper!

Motherhood teaches us not to worry so much about material things

Your children will probably make holes in the tablecloth, the shower curtain or the net curtains in your bedroom. They will break the screen of your camera or phone. They will spill juice or get some of that horrid, brightly-coloured play slime on the new carpet. They may set up a target in the living room, balanced on the back of the chair, and throw things at it. Sharp things. Things that make holes in the wall, as you will realise the next morning. Ahem, does it sound like I speak from experience? Whatever makes you think so?

A lot of the time at least, this will not be because of

premeditated, wilful naughtiness (though sometimes it will be, let's admit it). Usually they will not mean to cause trouble. Your children are just playing, learning, growing and exploring in their happy, clumsy way. You will have many opportunities to remind yourself that Jesus said, 'life does not consist in an abundance of possessions' (Luke 12:15). When things get broken or worn out we are reminded that our treasure is not here, and it is no use trying to live as though it is.

> Do not lay up for yourselves treasures on earth, where moth and rust [and children!] destroy and where thieves break in and steal, but lay up for yourselves treasures in heaven, where neither moth nor rust destroys and where thieves do not break in and steal. For where your treasure is, there your heart will be also. (Matthew 6:19–21)

We are often bombarded with images of perfect, beautiful houses, where everything is new, shiny and in place. But real life, especially with children, doesn't look like an Ikea showroom. There are so many things that are more important than our material possessions. Motherhood teaches us to let go of them and focus on what really matters. Your children's souls are worth infinitely more than the costliest item in your home.

Motherhood helps us to understand the fatherhood of God

Our relationship with our children can teach us many things about God's relationship to us as our heavenly Father. Thinking about the different ways in which we show love to our children can help us to grasp the extent of God's love for us:

- *He provides for us.* Jesus said, 'If you then, who are evil, know how to give good gifts to your children, how much more will your Father who is in heaven give good things to those who ask him!' (Matthew 7:11). Just as we seek to provide for our children, God provides for us. Have you ever tried to prepare a meal while a hungry toddler whines around your legs, making the job far harder? How often we do that with God! After telling him what we need, do we quietly trust him to act in his time, or do we keep moaning and whining about the situation? Think of the times when your children ask you for something that you know is not good for them. You refuse, because you are older and wiser! Sometimes God says no to something we ask for because he is so much wiser than us and knows that what we are asking for would not do us good.

- *He disciplines us.* '[The] LORD reproves him whom he loves, as a father the son in whom he delights' (Proverbs 3:12). Our children do not like to be disciplined, but we know that it is for their long-term benefit. Similarly, God sometimes brings trials into our lives to teach and train us so that we grow in righteousness.

- *He cares for and protects us.* When we sense danger, our instinct is to gather our children close and shelter them from harm. Jesus wept over Jerusalem, using maternal imagery to describe his feelings. 'O Jerusalem, Jerusalem, the city that kills the prophets and stones those who are sent to it! How often would I have gathered your children together as a hen gathers her brood under her wings, and you were not willing!' (Matthew 23:37). God wants us to find shelter in his love. The Psalmist prayed, 'hide me in the shadow of your wings, from the wicked who do me violence' (Psalm 17:8–9). Just as our children run to us for safety, we can run to our heavenly Father.

- *He welcomes and forgives us.* When our children let us down in their behaviour, we are sad and disappointed, but we don't stop loving them. We keep correcting, training, forgiving, welcoming and believing. Similarly, God doesn't give up on us when we mess up. Think of Jesus' story of the prodigal son, who took half of his father's fortune, went away and wasted it all. When he came to his senses and returned to his father's house, intending to ask to be a servant, his father saw him from a distance, ran to him, gave him the best robe, a ring and new sandals, then prepared a feast to welcome his son home (Luke 15:11–32). God is like that welcoming, forgiving father. Sometimes we are tempted to hide from him when we know that we have failed, just like Adam and Eve did in the Garden of Eden, and just like our children sometimes do when they know they have been naughty! Instead of hiding, we should run to God for forgiveness and grace.

Do your work for Jesus

'Truly, I say to you, as you did it to one of the least of these my brothers, you did it to me' (Matthew 25:40). The Lord sees your work, even if no one else does. He will reward you:

> Whatever you do, work heartily, as for the Lord and not for men, knowing that from the Lord you will receive the inheritance as your reward. You are serving the Lord Christ (Colossians 3:23–24).

Remembering this will help you to stay cheerful when you

are sweeping the kitchen floor for the fourth time that day, cleaning up sick in the middle of the night or comforting your accident-prone child for the eighth time in an hour. 'I appeal to you therefore, brothers, by the mercies of God, to present your bodies as a living sacrifice, holy and acceptable to God, which is your spiritual worship' (Romans 12:1). The work we do with our bodies can be an act of worship. Seeing Jesus as our employer while we are doing the work of raising our children can help us to keep growing spiritually.

> Mum Diary: December 2014
> **Faith**
> This morning I heard Y (age 3½) telling his sisters, 'God is looking after us. If a monster comes I'm sure he'll come and kill it.'

Accept the opportunities and limitations of this season of life

I realised a few years ago that throughout much of my life I had been looking forward to the next step, instead of seeking to make the most of the here and now for God's glory. As a school girl I couldn't wait to be at university. As a single student I couldn't wait to be married. When I was married I couldn't wait to be a mum. When I became a mum I thought, 'Well, what's next?' In some ways it is inevitable that in a fallen world, we have a longing for the next thing, something better around the corner. But that longing will never be fulfilled by earthly things. No stage of life is all roses. We will have different problems at different times. Each season comes with its own limitations, hardships, joys and responsibilities. We are citizens of heaven and our hearts are homesick to be with Jesus there. True satisfaction comes from knowing God and knowing that we are destined for heaven, while accepting and embracing his call on our life today. I love these verses in John 13:

> Jesus knew that his hour had come to depart out of this world to the Father, having loved his own who were in the world, he loved them to the end ... Jesus, knowing that the Father had given all things into his hands, and that he had come from God and was going back to God, rose from supper. He laid aside his outer garments, and taking a towel, tied it around his waist. Then he poured water into a basin and began to wash the disciples' feet and to wipe them with the towel that was wrapped around him. (John 13:1, 3–5)

Jesus knew where he came from. He knew where he was going. He was secure in his identity and secure in his destiny. This enabled him to accept the Father's present will for him and serve God right where he was, *at that moment*. Similarly, as Christian mothers, it is good to remember where we come from. We were created by God to glorify and enjoy him. It is good to remember where we are going. No matter how hard things are now, we are destined for a glorious eternity with Jesus and we would like our children to be there too. It is good to remember our identity. We are children of God and he has a plan for our lives today. He has work for us to do for him in our homes, right now. Keeping these things in mind can help us to accept the limitations of this relatively short time in which we are raising little children.

I went from being a single university student to being a pastor's wife and mother within an eighteen month period. It was a sudden life change and I occasionally struggled with resentment that I no longer had the freedom to go out in the evenings or to join in activities that had been a major part of my life up until that point. It hurt to be left out of the camaraderie of mission trips because I was at home with the baby. There are many activities that I love which I have had to put to one side to focus on what is important now.

Some days with small children are simply teeth-clenching, knuckle-down-and-get-through-it hard work. You'll want to throw that sixth explosive nappy at the person who tells you to enjoy them while they're little. I don't enjoy carrying huge amounts of baby equipment everywhere. I've forgotten what it is like to go out with a small handbag. I also don't enjoy the constant mess throughout the house, which multiplies faster than I can deal with it. Accepting the limitations of this life stage has meant accepting that my house will never look as nice as I would like it to, and it really doesn't matter. It helps to keep telling myself that people are more important than things. Here is a section from an email my mum wrote to me at a time when I felt particularly inundated by the endless chores and limitations of mothering:

> You have high standards in all you do and that's the way God has made you, but that makes you vulnerable to feelings of inadequacy and failure as the tasks are too numerous and too demanding for us. I heard your husband pray that your home should be a taste of 'heaven on earth,' and that's a wonderful thing to aim for. However, we must remember that we are still very much on earth. Jesus and the disciples were sometimes exhausted and in need of respite. It was always an uphill struggle for him. He suffered all those years in ways we cannot imagine: poverty, danger, temptation, misunderstanding, injustice, rejection, the constant clamour and demands of needy people, family tensions, physical and emotional and spiritual pain. 'A man of sorrows and familiar with suffering' (Isaiah 53:3). Daily life is a grind because we live in a

> fallen world, with fallen bodies corrupted by sin and years of inherited genetic deterioration.
>
> We find it so frustrating when we can glimpse perfection but cannot achieve it because there are not enough hours in the day or because our hands are tied up doing other vital things. Our bodies have limitations and we must recognise those limitations and accept imperfection here on earth. That may mean a less than clean house, a backlog of letters, a growing pile of washing and ironing, a scruffy garden. Few of these things will exist in 100 years' time. They will all be dust and rubble. 'For here we do not have an enduring city, but we are looking for the city that is to come' (Hebrews 13:14). You may sometimes feel you are sinking, going under. But in fact, you are persevering and putting up a fight. You may feel totally empty, drained, useless ... but you are still persevering. Perseverance is an integral part of Christian character and is only developed through testing experiences which sometimes appear beyond our ability to bear (James 1:2–4).

Slowly I have learned to embrace this season with its unique opportunities and limitations. The wise writer of the book of Ecclesiastes said, 'For everything there is a season, and a time for every matter under heaven' (Ecclesiastes 3:1).

I relish those evenings of utter quietness when my husband is out preaching somewhere interesting (or not so interesting!) and the children are asleep. To be brutally honest, children always give you a great and genuine excuse to get out of anything that you don't really want to be involved in! You will meet and bond with other mothers in a special way. You will have opportunities to talk about the Gospel in the park and at the school gate. If you learn to rest on God in those times when you feel overwhelmed, instead of going into panic mode, other mums will notice how calm you are and wonder what your secret is.

Try to make the most of each day you have with your children so that you won't look back with regret. I'm not talking about devoting all your time and attention to them or letting them become on idol. Of course, it is a good idea to have fun with your children when you can, but it isn't necessary, wise or even possible to spend every second of the day playing with them. You probably have far too many chores and other responsibilities. The important thing is that you are available for them. When they need you or want to show you something, stop what you are doing, bend down and give them your full attention so that they know they are important to you. Put that phone away! My siblings and I spent a lot of time playing in the garden when we were little. I don't have many memories of my mum playing with us, except on family outings. But we knew she was there. When we needed her she was our greatest comforter, our best listener, our biggest fan. You have opportunities to influence your children for good today, that may not come tomorrow. While I am looking forward to the greater amount of freedom (and tidiness) that will probably return as the children get older and more independent, I know that when we get to that stage, I'll probably miss the baby years.

So, embrace the opportunities you have now. Accept the limitations, the changing bags, the messes, and thank God for what he has given you today. Learn to rest on your heavenly Father even in the crazy moments, doing your work for Jesus. Walk in the freedom of forgiveness. This will help you to continue to grow spiritually in the midst of the challenges of motherhood.

4 Looking After Your Social Health

The fact that we are mothers doesn't mean that we should spend all our time and energy on our children, while neglecting relationships with other human beings. The Bible's many 'one another' and 'each other' verses demonstrate this need for varied social interaction. Here are a few: 'encourage one another and build one another up' (1 Thessalonians 5:11); teach and admonish 'one another in all wisdom' (Colossians 3:16); 'through love serve one another' (Galatians 5:13); 'Be completely humble and gentle; be patient, bearing with one another in love' (Ephesians 4:2 NIV). We are meant to live in community with others, putting these verses into practice, because in doing so, we bring glory to the God who is Love, and in whose image we were created. Love has always existed at the heart of the Trinity, and this should be reflected in our human relationships.

Social media

When we spend a lot of time alone with our children, it can be tempting to try to fulfil our need for social interaction by escaping into the world of social media. Online social networks can be a good way to stay in touch with friends and family far away, to share our faith with others and find out about events that are happening. However, there are several pitfalls that we need to be aware of.

Firstly, avoid the danger of being absorbed in a virtual world on your phone while ignoring your children, or simply wasting too much time on it. I once saw a heart-breaking video of a mother and her three-year-old daughter in a waiting room. The mother was engrossed in watching something on her phone while her little girl repeatedly tapped her and said 'Mummy, I'm cold' in a plaintive voice. She was completely ignored. In fear of repeating the same mistake, I have decided to avoid looking at my phone (especially social media sites), when I am with my children, unless we are looking at something together.

Secondly, remember to be careful what you share on the Internet, particularly regarding your children. Once pictures or personal information is out there, who knows who can access them or whether they can ever be totally erased? Children are not able to give their consent about what you put online, and so to avoid a great deal of future embarrassment for them, don't post comments or pictures of that potty training incident or the time you found them playing naked in the road. The golden rule of love applies here as much as anywhere else—how would I feel about someone sharing a photo of me like this? If in doubt, don't do it!

Thirdly, the sheer volume of information that we get about people's lives and environmental crises, forgotten war zones and suffering civilians can make us feel responsible for things that are outside of our control and sphere of influence. Being informed does enable us to pray and entrust problems to the

Lord, but I find that time on social media often leaves me with a vague sense of unease and dissatisfaction, burdened by too many problems that perhaps I did not really need to know about. Someone recently bought me a water bottle with this prayer written on the side of it, 'God, grant me the serenity to accept the things I cannot change, the courage to change the things I can, and the wisdom to know the difference.' We need to remember this whenever we are confronted with bad news.

Finally, online social media can give us a wrong impression of other people's lives, making us feel that they are all having a great time while we are just plodding on with our ordinary routine. I am writing this at the end of August and my Facebook feed is full of friends' lovely pictures of exotic holidays, barbeques and happy family days out. Of course, we tend to post the highlights and exciting things, not the mundane routine times or rainy days (although some people do like sharing what they had for breakfast). I enjoy seeing those pictures! But perhaps sometimes, like me, you also have a nagging feeling that, without the authenticity of day to day relationships, posting the happy things or a child's achievements could look like boasting, sharing troubles could look like moaning, and deep thoughts could look hypocritical or soppy!

It is natural to want to share our joys and trials with others, indeed Romans 12:15 commands us to care about the ups and downs in the lives of other people. I'm not saying that we should avoid online interaction, but it can never be a good replacement for real face-to-face relationships. We need to spend time with people with flesh on, people who are in our lives regularly, who know our strengths and struggles and are not hundreds of miles away. Some posts are better kept to a circle of close friends and family members. Jesus had different levels of friendship. From amongst the twelve disciples he had closer friendships with Peter, James and John, and John calls himself 'the disciple whom Jesus loved' (John 13:23). Jesus also had good friends in Lazarus, Mary and Martha of Bethany (John 11:5). I expect he shared things with them that he did not announce to the crowd. It is worth bearing this in mind when we are using social media. We also need to guard our hearts from wrong emotions of envy or comparison, remembering that what people post online is never the whole picture of their lives. Let's now consider some ways in which we can maintain beneficial, authentic relationships with other people while we have small children.

Marriage

The most important human being in your life is your husband (if you are blessed to have one). Spend time talking to him and find someone to babysit so that you can go out on a date once in a while. If there is no one to babysit, why not have a date night at home after the kids are in bed? Get a takeaway and something good to drink, light some candles, put some music on and pretend you are somewhere exotic.

I once went to a wedding and was slightly shocked when the preacher turned to the bride and said, 'Men want two things. Good sex and good food. If you give your husband those two things he will be happy.' Now, after more than a decade of marriage, I know that the preacher was right! Except that I would add one more thing. Respect. Respect is very important to a man. He needs to feel that his wife believes in him and trusts him. Virtually every passage

> Mum Diary: August 2017
> **Ceremony**
> The children just found a dead lizard in the paddling pool. They buried it, held a minute's silence and sang the French national anthem!

in the New Testament that speaks about marriage, mentions the need for a wife to respect her husband in loving, voluntary submission to him as the God-ordained head of the family.[5]

Of course, it takes two to make a good marriage. Your husband also has his responsibilities before God, but this is not a book for men. (I would be impressed if any man has managed to read it up to this point, through cracked nipples, childbirth wounds and femmale emotions!) We will not answer to God for our husband's behaviour, but we are responsible for our own. Be careful always to back up what your husband says in front of the children. They will respect their father if you respect him. If you disagree with something he says or does, talk to him about it in private later, being careful how you use your words so that you don't make him feel like an idiot. You won't succeed much at changing your husband by nagging. Deep, internal change is the Holy Spirit's job, not yours. Pray about the issue and trust God to lead your husband. Some things need to be discussed, but at other times you may realise that the quality of your marriage relationship is more important than pursuing the issue at stake. My mum often used to remind me and my brothers that 'it is to one's glory to overlook an offense' (Proverbs 19:11 NIV).

A word about sex. Your husband does not simply need to have his physical needs met, he also needs to feel desired by his wife. This is very important for a man's emotional wellbeing. Shaunti Feldhahn's book *For Women Only* deals with this and addresses many other helpful topics related to marriage and how men think. I know that after an action-packed mummy day when you have been covered at various moments in jam, flour, mud, playdough and bodily fluids, it is

5 See, for example, Ephesians 5:22–33, 1 Peter 3:1–7.

often hard to feel enthusiastic about sex. Your body is desperate for sleep. Sometimes you feel like you have been poked, grabbed and climbed on all day and you don't want anyone else to touch you. But making the effort to please your husband is always worth it. Loving him well will create a happy, peaceful home where your children feel secure. The intimate relationship between a husband and wife is meant to be a reflection of the love between Christ and his church (Ephesians 5:31–32). When we are lukewarm about the intimate side of our marriage, we are not accurately displaying the wonder of the Gospel. It can help to make a conscious effort to think about and pray for your husband during the day. Thank God for the good things you see in him and remember that you are a woman and a wife, not just a mother. It can also help you to switch out of mummy mode if you have a shower after the kids are in bed and change into something a little more alluring.

I know a lady who often advises women to 'know their man.' While sex, food and respect are extremely important to most married men, your husband may have other things he values more. A newly married friend told me that there was some tension in her marriage over differing priorities. My friend is an excellent cook, able to rustle up gourmet meals out of whatever happens to be in the fridge. But she struggles with tidiness. Her husband's mother, on the other hand, always kept her home immaculate and passed on her love of order to her son. Cooking was not her priority and her son grew up happy to eat food out of tins. All of us enter marriage with baggage and different expectations. It is a good idea to ask your husband what his priorities are, so that in busy times when you feel you cannot get everything done, you can focus on the main things that make home attractive for him. Know your man!

Perhaps someone reading this is a single mother. For one painful reason or another, the father of your children is no longer in your life. My heart goes out to you. I know it is not the same, but I have had just a little taste of the challenges and pressures you may face during the times that my husband has been away on long mission trips. God speaks tenderly in his Word about his special concern for women in situations like yours. Psalm 68:5 says that God is a 'Father of the fatherless and protector of widows.' Throughout the Bible there are many verses which speak of God upholding justice for single mothers and fatherless children.[6] He cares. I would encourage you to build a good support network. Your local church should be the best place to start …

Church

Whatever your marital status, be fully involved in your local Bible-believing church. Your church should be like an extended family, where people from all generations, with different cultural, ethnic and social backgrounds, can find a place to belong and serve others. At church you will find wise grandparents who can advise you, other mothers to exchange ideas with, and younger women looking to you for guidance and inspiration. You will find like-minded families to befriend and good role models, both male and female, for your children. There will be people there who can help you through difficult times, and others whom your family can help. You will receive Bible teaching to feed your soul, and spiritual food for your children, through Sunday school, children's clubs and worshipping with the rest of the church community.

The book of Hebrews tells us to 'consider how to stir up

6 See, for example, Psalm 146:9, Exodus 22:22–24, Proverbs 23:10–11.

one another to love and good works, not neglecting to meet together, as is the habit of some, but encouraging one another, and all the more as you see the Day drawing near' (Hebrews 10:24–25). It is always sad when families stop coming to church because they find it too hard to get out of the house with small children. They miss out on so much! Having a good creche room to take restless babies to certainly helps, especially if there are speakers relaying the service so that you can listen to the meeting while feeding and changing your baby. If your church does not yet have this facility, maybe you are the one who could get the ball rolling and encourage other members to consider making church easier for young families in this way. I have often visited churches where there was a creche room, but the speakers relaying the service simply weren't loud enough. As soon as a child made a noise or banged on a toy, the mothers couldn't hear anything. Creche room speakers need to be tested, not on a silent Friday afternoon, but when the room is full of toddlers and babies on a Sunday morning (just a little note for any church technicians who may be reading this!).

When we first moved to France, our little congregation met in a small shop front that used to be a barber's. There was nowhere to take noisy babies and I often ended up pacing the street with the pushchair. We eventually improvised a small creche room in the dark, damp basement, which was rather unpleasant and probably broke every health and safety rule out there. It was embarrassing when new families visited the church and were shown down into a dark hole when looking for somewhere to feed their babies! Eventually the church bought its own large building and included a fantastic creche room in the plans. It makes such a difference to parents. We should make it as easy as possible for families to come and hear the Word of God. But even if your church does not have good facilities for small children, don't give up going. The social and spiritual benefit your family receives will far outweigh the practical challenges in the long run. Remember, too, that even during the challenging years of early parenthood, going to church is not primarily all about what we can get out of it. It should also be about giving—giving praise to God and encouragement and service to other believers. Just by turning up you will be a blessing to others!

Think of ways to make Sundays special so that your children look forward to the Lord's Day each week. We generally have a treat for breakfast on Sunday, such as pains au chocolat, pancakes or brioche. We have some special Sunday DVDs. My parents only allowed my siblings and I to have sweets after lunch on Sundays. If we were given any during the week, we had to put them in special little bags with our names embroidered on them. (Although one year, my brother and I had some chocolate eggs on the bookshelves next to our bunk bed, waiting for Easter Sunday. A few days before Easter, we woke up early and scoffed the lot, hiding under our duvets. This is my first memory of feeling ashamed!) As I grew older, I loved the fact that I didn't have to do any school work on the Lord's Day. Church was a place where I knew I belonged, and Sunday was a day of freedom from the stresses of the week.

Family

Keep in touch with wider family. Spend time with them if you can, not just for your own sake, but so that your children can form bonds with their relations. I really miss my wider family in England. Although we can't see them as often as we would like to, when we do manage a visit it is always worth the cost of travel. I try to send photos, emails and birthday cards to keep in touch. My parents, siblings and their spouses have a WhatsApp group with us where we share all sorts of random things about our daily lives, some of which would not be appropriate to put on a more public social media platform. I try to remember to show the children the videos of their cousins. Skype is another good means of staying connected to loved ones.

Community and friends

Join a local mums and toddlers group if there is one. Could you start one if there isn't? In many communities you can find baby massage sessions or swimming classes for mothers and babies, which can be an enjoyable way to meet people. Go on day trips with other families. This is good fun for the children and helpful for you, as there are other adults around for you to talk to and to keep an eye on the little ones. And who knows what exciting snacks they may have put into their picnic basket to share or whether they will have some spare socks to lend your child who loves jumping in muddy puddles? Going on holiday with other families can also be good, provided you all get on well. Resident babysitters for an evening out during your holiday is always nice. Say 'yes' to people who offer to help you in practical ways. Look for opportunities to be involved in your community. Could you join the PTA of your local school or help to organise certain events in your village? This may not be a good idea if you already feel too busy, but if you feel isolated as a mother, looking for ways to volunteer in your local neighbourhood can be beneficial.

Hospitality

For many of us our home will be our principle sphere of influence, ministry and socialising during the years our children are small. You may not be able to get out to a lot of meetings, missions or meals, but you can use your home to serve and socialise. My hospitable, spontaneous, pastor husband is an expert at bringing home unexpected visitors, though in recent years he has got a little better at giving me some warning. I once prayed that I would always have enough food in the house to cater for unexpected guests. So far, God has always answered that prayer affirmatively! I usually find that as we seek to serve guests, we are the ones who receive the greater blessing. Visitors have invested in the lives of our children in so many ways.

Hospitality does not have to be complicated. It is welcoming people into your life and refreshing them by sharing what God has given you. To be hospitable means caring far more about blessing others than putting on a show. Sometimes a cold drink is all that is necessary, though of course every situation is different. Some guests will quickly make themselves at home, sit on the floor, play trains with your children and be happy to eat pizza with their fingers. In other situations, especially when welcoming people you don't know so well, a greater amount of preparation is necessary. It is a good idea to contact your guests to find out if there is anything that they don't eat before you plan what to feed them or do the food shop. This avoids the panic of having to conjure up something vegetarian or gluten-free at the last minute. Jesus spoke very directly about hospitality and who we should welcome into our homes:

> Mum Diary: September 2017
> **Fine cuisine?**
> This morning there was an awful burning smell in the kitchen. I found a popped balloon in the toaster.

> When you give a dinner or a banquet, do not invite your friends or your brothers or your relatives or rich neighbours, lest they also invite you in return and

> you be repaid. But when you give a feast, invite the poor, the crippled, the lame, the blind, and you will be blessed, because they cannot repay you. For you will be repaid at the resurrection of the just. (Luke 14:12–14)

Of course, this does not mean that we should never have friends round, but we limit our usefulness, as well as the blessing that could come upon ourselves and others, if we only ever invite friends. It is a good idea, if you have the space, to invite more than one single person, couple or family over at once. People who have attended your church for decades along with some newcomers, for example, or a mother from the neighbourhood and someone from church who you think she would click with. This allows other people to build friendships and deepen relationships, and they can talk to each other while you put the baby down for a nap or finish meal preparations. It will not necessarily involve much more work either. In fact, it can be a lot less work than if you had the same number of people round but on two separate occasions!

I find that my attitude towards my children, when I am preparing to receive guests, often reveals the motivation of my heart and whether I am really serving in love or seeking to impress and 'entertain.' If I am impatient with the mess or distractions that they are causing, it is likely that my heart is not right. This is a constant struggle, because my perfectionist artist-self wants everything to look as beautiful as possible and is often in conflict with being a kind and considerate mother. The New Testament tells us to offer 'hospitality to one another without grumbling' (1 Peter 4:9). It is a good idea to involve your children in preparations for guests. They can help to make a room look nice, put a rose from the garden in a vase, lay the table or chop things in the kitchen. This provides a lesson in serving others and helps you not to exclude them in your efforts to please your visitors.

A few years ago, I decided that I would never again apologise to unexpected callers about the state of the house. Hardworking mum, the Lord knows you work hard. Let the unexpected visitor think what they like! I want my children to feel happy and free to be creative at home. My oldest daughter loves making things out of junk, so her room is normally covered in little bits of paper, card and sticky tape. There is nearly always toothpaste smeared over the bathroom cabinet and sticky handprints on the glass doors. If you drop round at any time you will very likely find that the living room features a scruffy 'tent' made with dining chairs, blankets and clothes pegs and filled with toy cars, marbles and dinosaurs.

> Mum Diary: October 2016
> **Toddler trouble**
> Today, among other achievements, my two-year-old scrubbed the patio with her toothbrush, unravelled a whole toilet roll in the hallway, painted the sliding glass doors with muddy swirls on two sides of the house, tipped out some shimmery powdered make-up in my underwear drawer, and put her shoes on top of her baby sister in her cot. And I actually had a good day!

I once read a helpful sentence on a website: Hospitality 'picks up the house to make things pleasant, but doesn't feel the need to conceal evidences of everyday life.'[7] What a good balance to aim for. Yes, it is nicer for all if your toilet and hand towels are clean, and if you have made some effort to put a tasty meal on the table. Preparation speaks of care and love. But it is okay if your washing is out and there are still quite a few toys strewn over the floor. Students and other single

7 www.thegospelcoalition.org/article/why-hospitality-beats-entertaining

people, those who have left large families in other countries and those without children, are usually delighted to find themselves in a real family home which is bursting with the often messy evidence of little developing lives.

Sometimes people feel more at ease in an imperfect home than one where everything is spick and span. When I was seven years old one of my school friends was a little Greek girl. Our favourite game to play at her house involved digging up flower beds to look for pieces of pottery, which were, of course, part of a time machine. Her mum invited me to go with them to watch *The Little Mermaid* when it came out in the cinema. On the way we had to stop at the home of an aunt. The aunt's house was immaculate, with marble statues and polished surfaces everywhere. As a child I didn't know what to do with myself. We were given slices of chopped banana on plates with gold rims and told to eat them with a fork. I couldn't wait to get back in the car! I contrast this with the home of a single mother in her twenties who was a member of our church. I frequently walked round to visit her when I was a teenager. She often apologised for the state of her house, but I loved the atmosphere there and the fact that I could talk to her about anything. Where she saw an untidy desk, I saw that she had been sorting out her paperwork. The messy kitchen meant she had thought about what to feed me. I didn't see mess. I saw life and love.

So, do try to welcome people into your house even when your children are little. While some visitors will inevitably be more hard work than others, in general the conversations you have with your guests and the attention they give to your children will be a blessing to your whole family, as well as giving you contact with the outside world and meeting your need for social interaction. Hospitality, maintaining links with friends and family, and being involved in your church and community, as well as cultivating your marriage, will all help you to stay socially healthy during the early years of motherhood.

Part 2
An A–Z of tips for looking after your children and home

A is for Apples

When you have to take a toddler to a wedding, a funeral, a doctor's appointment or any other potentially awkward occasion when you really don't want them to make a scene, pack a pot of chopped, peeled apple. Produce this at the key moment when you see trouble coming—like when your toddler is getting restless and the doctor is about to take your blood pressure, or the bride and groom are making their vows. Apple will not make a mess on their wedding clothes or on the doctor's floor and as a bonus you may get comments about what a nice healthy snack it is and how well behaved your child is (chuckle quietly). Actually most toddler problems can be solved by producing food. Raisins and little cubes of cheese are also good foods for getting through situations in public that are not toddler-friendly. While we're talking about food, you may have noticed that children's behaviour deteriorates enormously when they have low blood sugar. My three younger brothers used to turn into wrestling, wriggling, wild things in the hour before dinner time and my children are exactly the same. Be aware of this, be

> Mum Diary: September 2013
> **Personification**
> Today Y (age 2½) and I looked at a book about trucks.
> Mum: 'What type of truck is that?'
> Y: 'Bin man truck.'
> Mum: 'Where do the bin men put the rubbish?'
> Y (pointing): 'There, in its bottom.'

realistic in your expectations of how long they will be able to wait to eat at that dinner party, and plan accordingly. A sandwich on the way in the car may make the evening more peaceful for everyone.

B is for Bumps, Bruises and Balance

Bumps and Bruises

Arnica cream for bumps and bruises really does work! If, like me, you regularly bash your shins on the open dishwasher and have lively children who frequently bump into things or each other, get some arnica cream. When you put it on as soon as possible after the accident, no bruise appears. I have tested this for several years and am convinced that it makes a big difference.

Keep a good supply of plasters of all shapes and sizes in your medicine cupboard, including some colourful ones designed to cheer up little ones. Sometimes a bright plaster can fulfil an emotional need to feel cared for, even if your three-year-old's scratch is barely visible. I also like to make sure I have a good supply of huge square plasters for the inevitable scabby knees. Paracetamol for all ages is another thing you don't want to run out of!

> Mum Diary: June 2011
> **Fearless explorer**
> 'Look Mummy, look! Issa crocodile!' announced S (age 21 months), coming into the house clutching a … dead lizard.

Balance

When talking about balance here I don't mean the physical attribute which can help you avoid using the arnica cream talked about above, although that type of balance is also useful, of course. Parents have to make decisions about all sorts of things. The devil often wants to mess up our lives by making us go to one unhealthy extreme or another. Finding a balance in practical areas of life is often the best way forward. 'Whoever fears God will avoid all extremes' (Ecclesiastes 7:18 NIV). You can probably think of many other situations where this is relevant, but here are some examples of how we can apply this helpful verse in practical areas of parenting:

- Don't be so worried about keeping your children safe that you never let them explore and take risks. On the other hand, don't be so laid back that you put their lives in danger through negligence.

- Some parents are obsessed with healthy eating, avoiding anything processed and panicking about added sugar. Others feed their kids junk food most days and don't really think at all about nutrition. A more balanced outlook would be to try to feed your children healthy food most of the time, but allow room for treats, remembering that there are more important things in life than food.

- You don't want to ignore your child's birthday so that they feel unloved, but neither do you need to spend a huge amount of money on excessive presents and outings. There are plenty of ways to make a day special without breaking the bank.

- 'All work and no play makes Jack a dull boy.' Children need to be educated and to have opportunities to develop their gifts, but don't go to the extreme of filling every second of their day with 'profitable' activities. Time for play is just as important.

- Some parents try to shelter their children away from the wider world to protect them from every bad influence, perhaps forgetting that sin often arises from within our own hearts (see Matthew 15:19). Others give their children huge amounts of freedom to visit other families' houses or wander around unaccompanied in the streets, perhaps forgetting that 'Bad company ruins good morals' (1 Corinthians 15:33). Neither extreme is helpful. We are to be in the world yet not of it (John 17:14–19). Yes, protect your children from unnecessary harmful influences. Talk to them about what to look for in a true friend. But allow them to visit school friends for set periods of time and encourage them to talk about their experiences and encounters in the world outside the home, so that they learn to process their environment through biblical glasses. Above all, pray for their protection and for wisdom as you make decisions.

> 'I searched—but there definitely was not
> a packet of instructions
> attached to my children
> when they arrived.
> And none has since
> landed in my mailbox.
> Lord, show me how
> to be a good parent.
> Teach me to
> correct without crushing,
> help without hanging on,
> listen without laughing,
> surround without smothering

and love without limit—
the way You love me.'[8]

C is for Chicken Pox, Clothes and Clutter

Chicken pox

My oldest daughter had chicken pox before she was two. I phoned my mum to ask what she thought the funny flat red marks with blisters on top could be. It was a very mild case. I chased my toddler around the room trying to dab calamine lotion on the spots and she just thought it was a great game. The rest of our children had chicken pox last year. My son brought it home from school, then twelve days later our three other girls came out in spots at the same time. They were utterly smothered in blisters and very miserable. Day four was the worst.

> Mum Diary: February 2018
> **What weather warning?**
> Temperature minus 5 degrees, bitterly cold wind.
> K (age 3): 'Mummy can we go to the beach?'
> Mum: 'No, it's too cold.'
> K: 'But we can wear our coats when we swim in the water.'

Friends recommended putting a bit of bicarbonate of soda in the bath. Another thing to try is pouring some oats into an old stocking and swishing this around in the bath. They make the water go a creamy colour and can soothe itching. Just don't forget to throw the oats away afterwards! Our oat sock somehow got hidden at the bottom of the basket of bath toys. After about a week there was a dreadful smell in the room. I cleaned the toilet, the bin and every corner several times,

---

8 Susan L. Lenzkes, *When the Handwriting on the Wall is in Brown Crayon* (Marshall Pickering, 1988).

but didn't think to look under the toys. I just couldn't find the origin of the stench. Another smelly week went by before I discovered the mouldy oat sock.

ViraSoothe Chicken Pox Relief Cooling Gel is worth a try, but my daughters found good old cheap calamine lotion more helpful for soothing the itching and drying up the spots. Give paracetamol to calm fevers and irritability, but ibuprofen should be avoided as it can lead to further complications. Lots of sympathy, nice things to eat and good DVDs will help your children get through it. Expect a couple of sleepless nights. The good thing with chicken pox is that it doesn't last long and very few people catch it twice! Remember to keep your child away from expectant mothers who have not had chicken pox, as it can cause damage to unborn babies. If you are pregnant, ask your doctor for advice.

Clothes

I sometimes feel like I am suffocating under piles of children's clothes. Dirty clothes waiting to be washed, holey clothes waiting for a stitch, too-big clothes waiting to be grown into, too-small clothes needing to be stored or given away. Here are some tips on how to clothe your children nicely but hardly spend any money. There are lots of ways of doing this and what works for you will depend on where you live and what facilities are available. Swapping bags of clothes with parents who have kids a bit older or younger than yours is great. We have a fantastic little shop near us which buys and sells second-hand children's clothes—very useful when you have a son who gets holes in his trousers in less than a week. (I like to keep some holey trousers for my son to wear on Saturdays at home when he spends a lot of time playing on his knees.) I know one mum who buys bags of clothes on eBay. You may have a freecycle or equivalent Internet group near you, where people are simply giving away the things they no longer need. Charity shops or car boot sales can be a good option. Go to charity shops in posh areas to find the best things! Children mostly grow at predictable rates, so I often buy bigger clothes in one year's winter sale ready for the following winter. Same with summer sales. Organise outgrown clothes, to be handed down to siblings or given away, into bags labelled with age and gender. Also write on the bag whatever is missing, for example, 'Age 6 boys, needs trousers and socks.' This helps you to know what to look out for without having to get everything out and rummage through it all.

With shoes I have found that you really do get what you pay for. Cheap shoes tend to fall apart within weeks. I have sometimes made shoes last a bit longer by sticking the front part of the sole back on with superglue, if the rest of the shoe still looks okay. It is often worth paying for leather ones at the start of a season or waiting for the sales to buy a good quality pair at a reduced price. Our shed features what I call my 'second-hand shoe shop,' basically some old pallets leaning against the wall, all the holes stuffed with shoes that are still in good condition, waiting to be passed down to siblings. Foot experts say that you shouldn't wear second-hand shoes because they will have taken on the shape of the previous owner's feet. Children grow so fast, however, that some footwear can be re-used, especially things like trainers and wellies which tend to keep their original shape. Most trainers can be washed in the machine with clothes and often come out looking as good as new. You can stuff them with newspaper to help them keep their shape and to dry out faster.

Clutter

I am in a constant war against stuff, or rather, unnecessary stuff. It creeps into our house at an alarming rate. Stuff spilling out of the letterbox and cluttering up the kitchen work surfaces, crowding out the bedroom cupboards and making other things impossible to find, tripping me up, stopping me being able to clean, and causing stress. Cuddly toys, paperwork, books, pens that don't work, drawings, bits found around the house that I am afraid to throw away even though no one is quite sure what they are or where they came from … A certain amount of clutter is inevitable in a family home but keeping it under control and in some kind of order is really helpful. Give things a place and encourage your children to put them back there (I haven't got very far in training my children to do this yet, but we are working on it). I want to be able to find those tweezers immediately when my child is hollering about a splinter, without having to wade through piles of other things first. For my sanity I need to have regular clear outs, donating things we no longer need and throwing away broken things that I know I'll never have the chance to mend. Decluttering is fashionable at the moment so there are lots of books about it, some of which are very extreme and probably best avoided. I read an excellent one recently called *Decluttering at the Speed of Life* by Dana K. White. It was realistic, funny, practical and contained many surprisingly helpful concepts that were easy to implement.

D is for Dreary Days

I don't remember minding the weather much when I was younger and childless. From what I have observed, the British are a lot more resilient than the French when it comes to braving the elements and following through on outdoor plans regardless. We happily say:

> 'Whether the weather be cold,
> or whether the weather be hot,
> we'll weather the weather,
> whatever the weather,
> whether we like it or not.'

Last year when we visited our previous church near Manchester for Easter weekend, my Mediterranean husband couldn't believe that the church went ahead with their planned Good Friday afternoon picnic and walk, despite torrential rain. He volunteered to take the little ones back to where we were staying (so they wouldn't miss their naps, of course), while I squelched through the mud with our older children and had a wonderful time eating our picnic and joining in the chocolate egg hunt under heavy clouds and dripping trees. Here in France, my son's football practice is often cancelled just for a little suggestion of wind, rain or mud. You will rarely find the French out walking in the rain.

Be that as it may, the more children I have, the more I find adverse weather bothersome. Bad weather on a non-school day means many hours of having to keep restless children occupied indoors, or if we do go out, it means fussing with raincoats, boots, umbrellas, runny noses, damp clothes, grimy pushchair wheels and mud. Oh, the endless mud! The plot on which our house is built used to be a vineyard, which makes the ground terrible for growing grass. In summer the mud patches are extremely dusty, but when it has rained and the children play outside, our patio quickly changes from peachy-orange to brown, and the mud is inevitably tracked indoors too, on little muddy knees, hands and feet. And this is not even to mention the difficulty of drying washing when the weather is bad! It cannot be denied that life is a lot easier for mothers of many when the sun is shining. I love packing up a picnic and taking the children outside for the day somewhere where they can be wild and free. Rainy days will come however, so here is a list of ideas, in no particular order, for keeping your children busy and happy when it is dreary and cold outside, and you do not feel up to an adventure in wellies:

- *Make an indoor obstacle course* using cushions, pillows, skipping ropes, plastic cups, masking tape on the floor and anything else you can think of.
- *Sing!* Go to YouTube and type 'Vacation Bible School Songs 2019' or another recent year. You will find a lot of lively (and slightly cheesy) American Christian songs for children, with action videos. Great for burning off excess energy!
- *Have an indoor picnic* on a rug, with favourite toys as guests.
- *Make houses out of chairs, tables and blankets.*
- *Invite friends round.* My mum has always said that children cancel each other out. You may actually get more peace on a rainy day if each child has a friend to play with.
- *Make a band* by giving toddlers upturned pots and pans, plastic bowls and wooden spoons to bash them with, if you can bear the noise. Rattles can be made of rice or pasta in plastic tubs.
- *Having a long play in the bath* with different beakers,

funnels and other objects to channel water through can be fun for children on a cold day.

- *Play cooking.* Put pasta, rice, dried beans and lentils in bowls on a tray, along with a few empty pots or saucepans and different sized spoons. This can get messy but at least it is dry mess that can be sucked up with the hoover.

- *Real cooking.* Small children from the age of about three years old love peeling, spreading and grating. Just be careful not to give them any tools that are too sharp. Melting chocolate and adding rice crispies or cornflakes, before spooning the mixture into cake cases to make crispy cakes, is always a favourite activity. You can try more ambitious cooking projects with older children.

- *Make a treasure hunt* that sends your children all around the house looking for clues. Younger children can have clues with simple drawings on them which lead them to where the next clue is hidden. Older children love little riddles and rhymes, such as, 'If you've had enough to drink, tip the water in the ______' or, 'If you want the next good clue, better look inside your sh___' You can find lots of examples of clues if you tap 'treasure hunt ideas' into Google. Sometimes I put a board game under a clue, with an instruction like, 'Play the game. The winner gets to lead the way to find the next clue.' This is really just a sly way to make the whole thing last longer. The 'treasure' doesn't need to be anything fancy … the children's snack, new colouring books and felt-tip pens or any other small toy.

- *Playdough.* This is wonderful stuff for children of all ages! You can make it yourself by putting the following ingredients into a saucepan (1 cup = 240ml volume):

  2 cups plain flour

  2 cups warm water

  1 cup table salt

  2 tbl vegetable oil

  1 tsp cream of tartar (optional but gives more elasticity)

  ½ small bottle (19ml) food colouring.

  Mix everything together over a low heat. Turn off the heat when it clumps together and pulls away from the sides. If it is still sticky, cook it a bit longer. You can save little plastic people from Kinder Eggs, cereal boxes or Happy Meals to use as 'dough men.' Toy animals, plastic knives and biscuit cutters are also good fun. Keep the dough in an airtight container.

- *Dressing up.* Collect odd items of clothing—funny hats, aprons, dresses, wigs, glasses etc. Children love disguising themselves and this can keep them occupied for a long time on a rainy day, especially if they start acting out a play.

- *Make models* out of junk from the recycling bin or give your child an old magazine, a pair of scissors, glue and some paper to stick pictures on. You can find hundreds of craft ideas on the Internet.

- *Bring out a toy that your children have not used for a while.* It is sometimes good to hide certain toys in the back of a cupboard for a month or two so that they seem new when your children see them again. Toys like dolls houses, Playmobil or Lego that encourage children to be creative and enter imaginary worlds are excellent.

- *An outing.* If you are desperate to get out of the house, but don't want to spend a fortune on a soft play centre or aquarium, you could try taking your children to the local pet shop, library or free museum. During our recent, bitterly cold February school holiday, I took my girls to an art gallery. My ten- and eight-year-olds loved looking at the pictures and making quick sketches of them. My lively three-year-old was not quite so impressed, however, and got some 'looks' from the people patrolling the quiet rooms, but even she enjoyed choosing her favourite picture in each room and posing for photos in front of paintings of ladies wearing pretty dresses. Needless to say, we did not stay in there for very long!

E is for Expectations

When entering a new or difficult situation with children, let them know how you expect them to behave before you go in. Children often live up to the expectations we place on them and sometimes bad behaviour only happens because they feel out of their depth.

We have two supermarket rules: 1. Don't touch anything and 2. Stay with mummy. As we pull into the car park, I always ask them to remind me what the two rules are. Quite often they'll add a few more too, like 'no running, no shouting, no screaming!' That's fine with me! If I don't do this, all sorts of unwanted items find their way into the trolley and I find myself searching for children under a row of jackets or behind the delicatessen. So, remind children how you expect them to behave before you go into the restaurant, the doctor's office or your great aunt Margorie's china-decorated living room. This will not guarantee good behaviour, but defining boundaries is especially important in unfamiliar environments.

I have just told you to inform your children of your high expectations, and now I am going to tell you not to expect too much (inwardly of course, not out loud)! We need to be realistic. There is some truth in the rather cynical phrase, 'Expect nothing and you won't be disappointed.' Our children are sinners. Remembering that will help us not to be unduly alarmed when they disappoint us.

> Mum Diary: June 2015
> **Great Expectations?**
> Mum: 'What might you expect to find in a beautiful garden?'
> Y (age 4): 'Snakes … and rats and mice.'

Another thing you should expect is a spillage at every mealtime. If you expect it in advance, you can react more calmly as you reach for the kitchen roll. I once heard of a man who was so in the habit of expecting spilt drinks that when it happened, he would say, 'Good, glad we got that over with.'

F is for Food and Fussy Eaters

Sometimes I can't believe how quickly food disappears in our house, and I don't even have teenagers yet! Everything now happens in larger and larger quantities. When you cook anything from scratch, be it casserole, cake or curry, make double or triple what your family will eat in one meal and freeze the rest. This is a massive time saver and means that you have a backup plan for days when you are too busy or too tired to cook. Just as when you have a newborn, it is useful, however old your children are, to have easy food options available for busy days—a few frozen pizzas with a bag of ready-washed salad, or other ready-made meals now and then, won't kill anybody.

I remember a period (a long time ago, honestly) when I couldn't bear any food that had skin on it, particularly tomatoes and peas. I once hid a mouthful of pea skins under the kitchen lino when my parents weren't looking. My dad would sit there patiently on Sunday afternoons while I chewed an increasingly dry mouthful of meat for hours. I could have got down from the table at any point, but the rule was that I had to finish my dinner if I wanted pudding ... and I always wanted pudding. My siblings and I learnt to enjoy virtually every type of food. We now have the same rule for our children, and it is a good one, as long as you are careful to give realistic portions for your children's ages and appetites. It is often better to give smaller portions, then serve seconds if your children need more. This also helps to reduce waste. Context is important too. When we are out at a friend's house or in a restaurant, the food may be unfamiliar or there may just be too much of it. In those situations, for the sake of common sense and a harmonious mealtime with your hosts, it is usually better not to insist that your child finishes his plate.

> Mum Diary: September 2010
> **Bon appétit!**
> Today I took a dead woodlouse out of S's mouth (age 12 months).

If you know that your child doesn't like something, put a tiny bit of it on their plate each time it is on the menu and expect them to eat just that mouthful. It may take many trials, but they will eventually get used to that food and start to appreciate it. Whatever you do, don't start cooking separate meals for your fussy eater. You will only confirm them in their fussiness, which will not do them or their future spouse any favours. Expect your child to eat what the rest of the family is eating. If they don't eat their dinner, don't offer snacks an hour later. Let them go back to their dinner. When people are really hungry, they eat! My parents sometimes used to set us a time limit when we were taking far too long over a meal. 'If it's not gone in twenty minutes you'll get down with no dessert.' We had no idea what a generous time limit twenty minutes really was, so we shovelled the food in fast. There must have been times when my siblings and I were grumpy about having to eat what we were given, but we are all grateful now that we were taught to enjoy the wonderful variety of foods that God has given us (well, as long as you don't offer me oysters, snails or woodlice!).

G is for Going Out

The simple act of leaving the house can be quite a feat when you have small children. As I have already mentioned, preparing bags and finding shoes the night before can be helpful, as can planning to leave fifteen to thirty minutes before you really must go. Another leaving-on-time tip is to put all your clocks five minutes fast and then try to forget about having done so. If you don't want to fast-forward every time-telling device, just do it to the clock that all the family tends to glance at before deciding whether or not they need to rush to get ready. This works even better if you can move the clock hands

> Mum Diary: August 2011
> **Scary animal**
> S (age 2), running away from next-door's ugly, snub-nosed little dog: 'Don't like that pig. It's eating me!'

secretly so that you are the only one who knows about it. Is that dishonest? I'll let you decide! Our clocks seem to get slower and slower—bad news when it comes to leaving on time, so my little fast clock trick is useful. If they start out a few minutes fast it keeps them from erring on the side of slowness for a month or two longer. Another reason this helps our family is that while I am a 'lets get to the airport really early to avoid panic' person, my husband is a 'why would you want to get there so early and waste time sitting around' person.

Whenever possible (and this obviously does not apply to catching planes or attending church), avoid stating a specific time of arrival to the people at your destination. I have learnt that a vague, 'We'll be there sometime around 10:30 or 11:00' leads to a lot less stress than if you say, 'We'll come at 10:30.' Although I do try to arrive at church on time, I hope that the times when I am late help to remind people that the pastor's wife is not perfect and should not be put on a pedestal.

Once you do get everyone out of the door, walking down the road can also be challenging, especially if you have some speedy racers who like to run ahead and some dreamy dawdlers who prefer to lag behind and inspect every little dandelion or hole. Here are some ideas that may be helpful:

- State your expectations for that particular walk before you set off. On dangerous roads, for example, make it clear that you expect everyone to stay together on the pavement.
- Get a responsible older child to hold a younger child's hand (stubborn toddlers sometimes like holding big sister's hand more than mum's).

- There are various combinations that work for transporting a baby and a toddler down the road: a double pushchair; baby in a sling and toddler in a single pushchair; baby in the pushchair and toddler on a buggy board. If you have a three year old who tends to run into the road at unpredictable moments, you could try attaching him to the pushchair with reins. I get funny looks doing this in France, but reins are more popular in the UK and are a good, safe option.
- I have a friend who sometimes takes a three-wheeled scooter on outings for her two-year-old instead of a pushchair. The handles are at a comfortable height for an adult to push if the child gets tired. We often take a scooter on family walks to help anyone who gets tired to keep up.
- If your children are all lagging behind, try turning the walk into a game. You could try:

  1.Run to a tree … run to a car … run to the stone chicken … run to the next lamppost.

  2 Who can walk along the pavement only treading on cracks? Or who can avoid all the cracks?

  3.Who can find a treasure (or pretty leaf or stone, etc.)?
- My sister-in-law successfully bribed eight children over a mountain in the Lake District by promising them jelly tots when they got to the next landmark. While I would not recommend bribery as a regular parenting technique, there are certain situations in which rewards can be very useful … a few sweets or raisins in your pocket can sometimes save the day. My sister made up a cute song when she was about three-

years-old: 'Put a chocolate bar in your handbag [x3] and you'll be happy after all.' You may be the one who ends up needing the chocolate!

H is for Hope and Healthier Snack Ideas

Hope

The Bible says that love 'hopes all things' (1 Corinthians 13:7). In many ways it is natural for mothers to keep hoping for the best for their children. One often hears stories of mothers continuing to hope and pray for their wayward adult offspring, long after the rest of the world has given up on them as a lost cause.

There will be times when you feel discouraged and a little hopeless about something related to a child. Parenting is a long-term task in which you do not always see immediate, visible results. In today's world we like quick fixes, a sense of achievement, an easy solution, efficiency and productivity. It is easy to feel that the time we spend correcting, training, comforting, encouraging and guiding our children, is not making any difference. This is not true. We need to live in faith and hope, believing that the seeds we sow in our children's lives will eventually bear good fruit. 'And let us not grow weary of doing good, for in due season we will reap, if we do not give up' (Galatians 6:9). The hugs we give sow seeds of security. The truth we sow will guide our children in their future decisions. The time we spend on a day out with them may not seem to have achieved anything tangible, but we have hopefully sown happy memories and close family bonds that are worth their weight in gold. When a farmer plants a crop, he knows that it will not bear fruit immediately. He must wait patiently and continue watering and caring for those seeds. The harvest will come in due time. Proverbs 31 says of the wise woman, 'Her children rise up and call her blessed' (Proverbs 31:28). They may not call her blessed while she is potty training, teaching them not to be fussy over food, or training them to respect authority. It is often only when they are older that children realise and appreciate all that their mother taught them. We need to live in hope, with our eyes fixed on a long-term goal.

When I paint a picture, I don't like people looking at it until it is finished. Works of art can appear unattractive or messy throughout the various necessary stages of production. No artist wants someone to make a judgement about something half-done. Our children are also works of art in progress, as indeed we all are. I have never liked people making comments about a child's behaviour as if that child is trapped in the moment, labelled as naughty or temperamental for the rest of their life. This vision leaves no room for grace or hope. Children grow out of many childish habits. Prayer and godly discipline will also pay off in the end. Never lose hope, just keep sowing good seed and adding those beautiful brushstrokes to your child's life.

I have recently found some encouraging promises for God's people in the book of Isaiah. For example:

> for like the days of a tree shall the days of my people be, and my chosen shall long enjoy the work of their hands. They shall not labour in vain or bear children for calamity, for they shall be the offspring of the blessed of the Lord, and their descendants with them. (Isaiah 65:22–23)

David wrote that 'the steadfast love of the Lord is from

everlasting to everlasting on those who fear him, and his righteousness to children's children, to those who keep his covenant and remember to do his commandments' (Psalm 103:17–18). Remember God's promises, hold on to them and quote them back to the God who gave them, as you pray for your children. When God fills our hearts with hope, there is no room left for fear.

Another thing that can make mothers feel hopeless is seeing how quickly their practical work around the house is undone. I don't know about you, but I can generally cope with messes that are a by-product of a necessary or creative activity, such as eating or painting. It is the pointless messes that really get to me! A few days ago, I realised that my nearly four and nearly two-year-olds were too quiet. I went to investigate and gasped at the sight of their bedroom. They had emptied out every drawer and strewn the clothes all over the place. It took me about fifteen minutes to fold everything up again. I was not a happy mummy and my little ones had a stern talking to. The next day, they did exactly the same thing, except that this time my three-year-old was guiltily stuffing clothes back into drawers as I opened the door. Discipline time! The first time their actions could be excused as childish foolishness, requiring guidance and a warning. The second time it was wilful defiance, requiring correction. I felt like crying as I manoeuvred my now heavily-pregnant body down to the floor and folded up the clothes all over again. At that age, children can make a mess in an instant, but are unfortunately too young to fold clothes properly by themselves.

Every mother can think of examples like this, whether the mess is intentional or not. You hoover and dust the living room, then someone comes along with a biscuit, leaving crumbs everywhere and smearing chocolate on the sofa. You change the bedsheets then your child wets himself that very night, for the first time in months. Even when you know that performing these repetitive tasks is necessary, glorifying to God, a service for Jesus, and for your family's health and long-term benefit, you can still feel a sense of futility and frustration. It is helpful, occasionally, to focus on a project that will not be destroyed by the time the next meal comes around. Doing something that does have a visible, lasting result can cheer mothers who feel drained by the endless round of the same old chores. Planting bulbs that will come up every year, clearing out and organising a cupboard that is out of the reach of little hands, or making something beautiful that will last, are all examples of this. But don't make the mistake of thinking that your invisible work of loving and training is any less important!

Healthier snack ideas

A few years ago the tooth fairy was rather unhappy that quite a few of the milk teeth she found in our house had cavities in them. We bought electric toothbrushes for the older children, switched to a strawberry flavoured toothpaste that contained more fluoride than the average French brands, and decided to make an effort to find tooth-and-child-friendly snacks. Here are some ideas:

Breadsticks dipped into soft cheese.
Cheese cubes and crackers.
Lightly salted popcorn.
Raw nuts or salted peanuts (obviously not for little children).
Rice crackers.
Cherry tomatoes.
Cucumber, carrot or bell pepper sticks.
Fresh fruit.

Bread with savoury toppings—peanut butter, marmite, etc.
Bananas chopped into three, with a lolly stick poked down the centres, rolled in Greek yoghurt and cinnamon and frozen.
Tinned chick peas, flageolet beans or red kidney beans, with a little cumin and salt.
Boiled eggs.
Pita bread dipped in hummus.
Cooked pasta shapes.

I is for Independence

The more you can encourage your children to be independent in little everyday tasks, the easier your life will be! This is particularly helpful if you have a lot of little people to care for. It is a relief when some of them can put on their own shoes and fasten their own seatbelts. Of course, children develop at different rates and are ready for each step of independence at different times. I recently accompanied my son's class to their swimming lessons and was surprised at how many of the six-year-olds didn't know how to put their own socks back on! I imagine it is because their parents have always done it for them. Allow your children to figure things out for themselves sometimes before you rush in to help them.

I sometimes have a mental list of 'independence goals' for my children during the summer holidays when we have more time. For example, I might aim to teach my daughter to wash her own hair, my son to do up his shoelaces, and my two-and-a-half-year-old to get her little step and sit on the toilet by herself. Small things can save you huge amounts of time on busy days. We live in a quiet French village, ten minutes' walk from the village school. This year we decided to allow our ten, eight and six-year-olds to walk home alone together after school a couple of days a week. This not only makes life easier for me, because I don't have to rouse their little sisters from their naps early, it is also, I hope, preparing them for the future when they will have to travel further afield to school on their own. We made sure that they knew the rules first: stay together, don't ever get in a car with anyone and be careful crossing roads. Hand responsibilities over to your children little by little as you think they are ready. You are preparing them to fly!

Another idea I have found helpful is giving the older children a checklist of things that they must do on Saturday morning, usually including homework, music practice, hair wash and one simple chore like feeding the guinea pig. I used to write these lists on slips of paper with their names on the top but have recently purchased a whiteboard which is more effective. They enjoy looking for the next thing on their list and ticking off the boxes. It saves me having to nag them to get things done. They are responsible for initiating the tasks, though of course I am there if they need some help. (My toddler recently scrawled on the whiteboard with a permanent black marker. I thought those marks would never come off but discovered by accident that if you draw over the marker lines with a proper whiteboard pen and then wipe them with kitchen towel, they do disappear! Who's brave enough to see whether whiteboard pens get permanent marker off other surfaces? Not me!)

J is for Jokes and Joy

Jokes

Being a mum is hard work. It can be helpful to learn to see the funny side of little things that go wrong and not take yourself too seriously. 'A joyful heart is good medicine' (Proverbs 17:22). Write down the hilarious things that your children say. Everyone will like looking back on them. Enjoy your family clown if you have one, and most families do. Think about ways to make your children and husband smile. Buy an age-appropriate joke book for your child who has just learnt to read. Watch a comedy occasionally to lighten your mood. My children love watching old Laurel and Hardy films with their dad! The Proverbs 31 woman 'laughs at the time to come' (Proverbs 31:25), because she trusts God instead of letting herself become anxious. If we do all sorts of sacrificial things for our children, but with a sour face and a begrudging spirit, life will be miserable for everyone.

> Mum Diary: February 2014
> **Word play**
> Y (age 3), looking at a book: 'What's that, Mummy?'
> Mum: 'It's a mammoth, like a really hairy elephant, but now they're extinct.'
> Y: 'It stinked?'
> Mum: 'No, it's EX-tinct. That means they all died and they don't exist anymore.'
> Y: 'It stinked? It was all yucky and smelly?'

Joy

There will, however, be days when difficult circumstances make it impossible or inappropriate to joke around. In those times, the reality of our faith is tested, and we have an opportunity to learn what it means to 'rejoice in the Lord always,' even in suffering (Philippians 4:4). Christian joy is one of the fruits of the Holy Spirit, stemming from a firm assurance that God is in control and has a wonderful plan for us. By grace we can make the *decision* to rejoice in God's love, goodness and promises, walking by faith instead of by sight.

This enables us to soar above our circumstances and maintain that inner joy which those who do not know God cannot understand.

K is for Keep it Simple

I enjoy planning events, showing hospitality and being creative. The temptation is to take on too much. It is helpful to take a step back after making plans and ask yourself whether there is a way to simplify things. This may mean a simpler menu using more ready-prepared ingredients, buying a cake instead of making one during a busy period when time seems more valuable than money, reducing your ideas of what you aim to get done in a day, abandoning certain plans that are simply not realistic in this season of life, or going to the local park instead of somewhere far away if you are already tired. Sometimes having more time to do simple things ends up making everyone happier than if you attempt something elaborate. As we have seen, it can be efficient to get a lot of errands done at once in one area of town, but there may be days, such as when you are accompanied by a teething baby, when it is wiser just to focus on doing the most important thing and getting home again quickly!

Raising children can often seem complicated and daunting. You can feel pressure for them to be involved in hundreds of activities, or to buy certain things for them that other children in your neighbourhood have, but their basic needs are really very simple. I recently watched *The Inn of the Sixth Happiness*, a not very true-to-life representation of the story of Gladys Aylward, missionary to China. In the film, she comes across a heartless beggar woman who has a crying baby lying naked on the floor next to her, a baby donated by another beggar. Gladys buys the baby off her for sixpence. Her companion asks,

'What are you going to do with her? What do you know about babies?' I like the way Gladys replies; 'What is there to know? When they're dirty you wash them. When they're hungry you feed them. We'll find an inn and do both.'[9] Often caring for children is really as simple as that. Your motherly instincts will usually tell you what your child needs. Keep life simple.

L is for Laundry

To keep clothes looking nice and avoid the rather depressing sight of dirty-looking grey vests or shirts that were once white, it is a good idea to separate whites from colours. The bigger your family, the easier it is to do this as you nearly always have enough of one type of colour to make up a load.

Rub stains with Vanish Stain Remover and cold water before putting your clothes in the wash. For stains that are mostly just grease, apply a bit of washing up liquid and hot water before the clothes go in the machine. If clothes come through the wash and still look stained, I find that the sun is an excellent stain remover. Hang any stained items in a place where they will get as much natural light as possible. Even on some cloudy days, there are often enough UV rays coming through to bleach those stubborn stains out, though I confess that this works better in southern France than it did in northern England.

> ✎ Mum Diary: August 2016
> **Slavery?**
> Today Y (age 5) helped me water the garden with paddling pool water. He suddenly said, 'I like working. When I grow up, I want to be a slave.'

While we are on the subject of removing unwanted marks, magic eraser sponges are the most amazing cleaning product I have discovered. Not for laundry, unfortunately, but for

9 *The Inn of the Sixth Happiness* (20th Century Fox, 1958).

virtually every hard, washable surface in the home, particularly painted doors and walls. In a house where there are children, walls frequently get covered in scuff marks from shoes and hard toys, handprints and toddler scrawls. You just wet the sponge and rub the mark gently. All sorts of things that do not come off with normal cloths can be made to disappear. The sponges sometimes leave a bit of white powder behind which you can wipe off with a damp cloth. Also WD-40 is amazing for removing residue left by sticky tape and labels.

I don't have a tumble dryer so I dry everything on a washing line or airer. To avoid ironing but still have clothes that look ironed, set the washing machine on the lowest spin speed you dare to go for, according to the weather. In sunny, windy weather, go for a low spin speed. I have found that 600 is best for crease-free clothes. Peg up t-shirts and tops by the very bottom corners, as near to the edge as possible, then give them a good stretch in all directions. Hang trousers by the ankles using two pegs for each leg, again folding over as little material as possible and stretching in all directions. Hang dresses by the shoulder seams or the base, depending on the style. Shirts can be dried on coat hangers or hung by pegging along the natural fold of the collar. The stretching/smoothing part is important and only takes a few seconds. The weight of the water, combined with gravity and wind, will iron your clothes for you! This works best on a washing line. But you can also peg clothes like this on an airer with good results, instead of folding them double. Just don't put your machine on a very low spin speed on sultry, windless, damp days or your clothes may just go smelly. On days like that, spin clothes on 1000 and hang in the same way, inside or outside. Some cotton dresses and shirts have to be ironed no matter how you dry them, but I find that this works for most things.

A few years ago, I bought a battery-powered lint remover which is fantastic for getting rid of those annoying bobbles that form on jumpers and cardigans. It has given a new lease of life to many items of clothing that would otherwise have looked rather worn out. Lint shavers are easy to buy online.

M is for Money

Although I have already mentioned some money-saving tips, such as how to clothe your children cheaply and ideas for outings that won't cost you much, money is a subject that worries many parents and deserves its own section. People often wait a long time to have children today, feeling that they first need to have a stable career, a big house with a garden and a fancy nursery. Of course, God leads some people to a good spouse later in life than others but sadly, some couples focus on other ambitions for so long before they think of starting a family, that when they finally get around to it they find that their bodies have passed ideal childbearing age and it is a lot harder to conceive than they had imagined. It is however a myth that having children is expensive. Having a nice house, garden and nursery is not wrong in itself of course, but neither are these necessary requirements for bringing a baby into the world. A child's needs are really very simple. They need love, food, clothes, a place to sleep and opportunities to learn. Children are a wealth and blessing in themselves, always seen in Scripture as a gift from God.

> Behold, children are a heritage from the LORD,
> the fruit of the womb a reward.
> Like arrows in the hand of a warrior
> are the children of one's youth.
> Blessed is the man
> who fills his quiver with them! (Psalm 127:3–5)

Remember that children do not need everything all at once. You can wait four or five months before they are ready to move from a moses basket (or cardboard box!) to a cot. You only need a highchair once they reach the age of about seven months. Before that they can sit on your lap, in a 'bumbo' or bouncer chair to eat solids (although a child must be completely upright if the food is not puréed). God will provide for you at each stage of your child's development. Learn to trust his provision. He owns 'the cattle on a thousand hills' (Psalm 50:10). As Jesus said, if God clothes the grass of the field with beautiful flowers and feeds the birds, he will also take care of your family's needs. 'But seek first the kingdom of God and his righteousness, and all these things will be added to you' (see Matthew 6:25–34). The Psalmist writes, 'I have been young, and now am old, yet I have not seen the righteous forsaken or his children begging for bread' (Psalm 37:25). The One who created you and knows all your needs will provide, step by step.

Here are a few more money-saving tips that I have found helpful:

- Baby equipment is expensive if you buy it new, but since babies grow faster than they can wear things out, an abundance of second-hand baby equipment is out there on freecycle, eBay, in charity shops and quite possibly in your friend from church's garage, ready and waiting to be offered to you.
- Having tried several highchairs, I believe white Ikea ones are the best and I know many mothers who agree! They are cheap to buy, easy to clean (you can even put the tray in the dishwasher) and if one part gets worn out, you can replace just that bit. The legs are also less

spread out than those of some highchairs, so you don't trip over them quite as much.

- Find out about, and claim, all the benefits that you are entitled to, for example child benefit and child tax credits.
- Breastfeeding is obviously the cheapest way to feed a baby, but the NHS also offers Healthy Start vouchers to help parents who receive certain benefits to buy infant formula, as well as fruit, vegetables, milk and vitamins. For more information and to see if you qualify, visit the website: www.healthystart.nhs.uk
- Using washable nappies can save a lot of money in the long term, particularly if you use them for more than one child. Shop around before buying anything. There are many different sorts appearing on the market. Ask your midwife about washable nappy trial schemes. I ordered a whole set of bamboo nappies in two sizes before my first daughter was born and have used them for all of my children, though progressively less for each child, partly due to having less time and partly because the elastic and velcro parts are wearing out and I don't want to buy a new set! The disadvantages of washable nappies are that they have to be changed more frequently to avoid leaks, they are bulkier under clothes and you obviously have to get them washed and dried. I have often found it good to use washables when we are at home and disposables when we are out. Washables are particularly economical and practical for newborns, as they fill their nappies so often with small amounts of milky poo. Once your child is learning to walk, bulky washables are less

comfortable for the child between their little, wobbly legs, and may not hold the larger amounts of urine, especially at night.

- Learn to cook from scratch if you haven't yet done so. My mum taught me to make a few things before I left home and I took some favourite recipes with me, but I mostly learnt to cook through trial and error (as my poor husband could testify!). Jamie Oliver's books are a great place to start as he outlines the recipes so clearly and mostly uses simple ingredients that are easy to find. You can save money by cooking in bulk and freezing, using cheaper seasonal produce or whatever happens to be on promotion, and including vegetarian meals regularly in your diet. I like to pad out meat dishes such as spaghetti bolognaise, with all sorts of vegetables chopped small, such as carrots, peppers, courgettes and red kidney beans. This makes expensive meat go further and is good for our health too. If you manage to get to the supermarket or street market near closing time, you may find lots of things reduced in price, some of which you can freeze for another day.
- If you have a garden, why not plant fruit trees as well as growing your own herbs and vegetables? Children love planting things and it is very rewarding to harvest your own crop. Making your own compost out of biodegradable kitchen and garden waste is a good idea and can make you feel less guilty about any food that your children waste. It helps to think that one day that messed around pasta salad or apple crumble may be reincarnated as a vegetable! I made my compost bin out of four old pallets from a DIY store, tied together with fence wire.

- Keep birthday celebrations cheaper by making your own birthday cakes and organising fun birthday parties at home, with traditional party games that children love, instead of buying expensive birthday party deals at fast food restaurants or play centres.
- Learn to do your family's haircuts yourself. If you have boys, it is worth buying electric hair clippers. My husband likes to have his hair trimmed every three weeks. Haircuts are expensive in France, so we have saved a fortune doing them at home. The clippers paid for themselves after just two trims. The first time my husband asked me to cut his hair was four days before our wedding! I had never cut anyone's hair before and was worried about making him look ridiculous for our big day. He was far calmer, however, and simply told me step by step which length attachment the hairdresser would use where. Thankfully it turned out okay. Our girls all have extremely curly hair. I took one daughter to a hairdresser a few years ago so I could watch how the professional tackled her long locks and have tried to copy her technique. The good thing with curly hair is that even if I make a mess of it, it doesn't really show. If your girls have straight hair you may have to be a bit more precise, but simple trims should be manageable. If your children generally hate hair washes or haircuts, a helpful tip is to give them a dry flannel to hold over their eyes.
- Walk to local places whenever possible instead of automatically jumping in the car. It is good for your health, the environment and your budget!
- Get yourself a reusable menstrual cup. Over the years

this will save you a huge amount of money on sanitary products. Some women find that they can use the menstrual cup on its own. Others find that it leaks a bit on the heaviest days of their period and they need to use a pantyliner with it. There is no need to buy an expensive brand. The cheaper menstrual cups, easily available from online retailers for a couple of pounds, are just as effective. Menstrual cups usually come in two sizes, with the larger size being appropriate for women who are over thirty or who have given birth vaginally. You could try washable pads too, if you're brave enough to give yourself extra washing!

- Try using an Ecoegg for washing clothes. The lack of harsh chemicals makes it ideal for sensitive skin. I have found that it works well for washing loads of up to five kilos. The perfume is very light, so you may want to add fabric conditioner. If you put in a bigger load, the instructions recommend using a second Ecoegg at the same time, or you can compromise by adding a bit of your usual washing detergent. Otherwise, the sweaty armpits of men's shirts and very dirty socks do not come out as clean as one could wish. The Ecoegg company also make economical and ecological stain remover and fabric conditioner which you may like to try. Another option is to look online for recipes allowing you to make your own laundry detergent and other household cleaning products. Most of them involve vinegar and bicarbonate of soda.
- Save on water bills by installing a water butt in your garden to collect rainwater from the roof. This water can obviously be used on the garden, but also for cleaning the car, the windows and the pet's cage. In

fact, it can be used for washing anything that doesn't require the water to be perfectly clean. Try to re-use water where possible. Paddling pool water or water from the baby bath can also be used to give plants a drink. Water in bottles left over from a picnic and unpleasantly warmed by the sun can still be used as kids' painting water, or to boil eggs, soak pots and pans that are encrusted with baked-on food, soak stained baby clothes, fill the iron (if your water is soft enough) or in the mop bucket. Putting two or more small children in the bath together can also save on water.

- Many machines around the home continue to use electricity even when not functioning. Some radios, TVs, computers, printers, speakers, washing machines, phone and toothbrush chargers and dishwashers all continue to use electricity if left on standby. Anything with an LED light still showing is costing you money. Where possible, unplug machines that you are not using. Make sure the dials on dishwashers and washing machines are turned to the off position after use. You can save energy by turning your thermostat down and putting on an extra jumper, and of course, remembering to turn lights off. Put lids on pans to keep the energy in when you are boiling food, and only boil as much water in the kettle as you really need. Tumble dryers use enormous amounts of energy, so dry washing on a line or airer whenever possible. Fill your dishwasher and washing machine to maximum capacity to make the most of the energy and water used.

I am reluctant to say a great deal about the issue of whether or when to go back to paid employment after having children. Each family's situation is different. It is not my place to judge anyone else's decision and this is a topic that has already been thrashed out by many good Christian writers. I know and admire some lovely Christian women who successfully combine part-time work with the care of young children, though I also know that they are often tired and struggle with the difficult act of juggling childcare, work and home responsibilities. Perhaps your husband feels called to stay in an area where housing is expensive, and you feel you have no choice but to work to help pay the rent or mortgage. Maybe you are a single mum and are obliged to work to provide for your children. Perhaps you are a trained nurse and would lose your registration if you didn't keep working. Maybe your husband is studying, cannot work for health reasons, or has been unable to find work for a long time. Each of us will have to answer to God for our decisions and choices. The Lord knows whether we are motivated by greed, genuine need or something else entirely.

One aspect to consider is whether we are seeking to find our main identity through the work we do, and the labels placed on us by society, or through who we are in Christ. Our sense of self-worth and identity is misplaced if we are relying on our achievements outside (or inside) the home to prove something to others. Living for Christ and letting his love shine through us should be our main motivation, whatever choices we make in this area. Of course, some jobs are easier to combine with motherhood than others, and whether or not you have helpful members of your wider family nearby can also be a factor.

Many women are delighted to leave the pressures of a routine, difficult job to care for their children, but for others it is more of a struggle. I know several women who had excellent, enjoyable jobs before they became mothers, but their work outside the home demanded so much of their time and attention that they knew it was not compatible with being a present mum. Their decision to leave their job was part of the way in which they 'lay down' their own life for the sake of giving life to others (John 15:13). This is not a popular concept in our culture, but one that is at the heart of Christianity and often leads to deeper joy in unexpected ways. One mother I know, who has always dreamed of becoming a nurse, recently wrote this on social media:

> So last week I quit uni (well for a while ... a year at least) and I feel so good and so free! I was wrestling with doing it for a while but couldn't make up my mind and didn't follow my gut and my heart. Instead I listened to the pressure of the "world"! Thought I should be doing something else than what I am currently called to do, and that is to be the best, most present and in the moment Mum I can be. I DO NOT want to miss a moment with my kiddies. They are only little for so long and I want to live with no regrets. I don't want to look back in fifteen years and wish I just sacrificed that job, uni, house, holiday, clothes, things (that let's be honest do not bring happiness) so that I didn't have to miss out on seeing my kids grow up. Everything else can wait![10]

Mum Diary: April 2011
Affection
Today S (19 months) put her sticky little arms around my neck and said, 'I yuv you' for the first time.

Choosing to be a 'stay-at-home mum,' reducing your

10 Used with permission.

working hours, or re-arranging your timetable so that you can spend more time at home, may of course involve some financial sacrifices or changes, especially if you are used to living on two incomes. You may need to move to a cheaper area or go on fewer holidays, for example. But I say again that God will provide everything that you really need. I do believe that making the choice to give the best part of your time, energy and self to your family, if you have that option, will make you far richer in other, more important and lasting areas—a better quality of family life, more time with your children, a greater sense of security for them, a wealth of memories, and more opportunity to invest in lives instead of in things. By providing your own childcare, gardening, cleaning and cooking, you contribute to the financial and emotional needs of your family in a huge way.[11] I have never met a woman who regretted being a 'full-time mum' while her children were little. On the other hand, I have encountered many who have told me that they regret giving so much time to their careers, to the neglect of their families.

God has equipped women with special nurturing abilities. In the book of Titus, Paul encourages young women to 'love their husbands and children, to be self-controlled, pure, working at home, kind, and submissive to their own husbands, that the word of God may not be reviled' (Titus 2:4–5). It is clear that the wise woman of Proverbs 31 put her family's needs first, even though she was also a businesswoman with other responsibilities. Children grow up

> Mum Diary: March 2012
> **Poison**
> Today dad showed S a bottle of ant-killer with pictures of ants on the front of it. He asked S (age 2) what they were and she said, 'The things in my hair!' She has never yet had nits.

11 See www.mothersathomematter.co.uk.

incredibly fast. Whether or not you have to go out to work, try to be available for your family as much as you can. Your children need your love, time and attention more than they need your money. I like the song that Bert (Dick van Dyke) sings in the *Mary Poppins* film, encouraging the work-obsessed father to notice his children more. It is a good lesson for us all:

> You've got to grind, grind, grind
> At that grindstone
> Though childhood slips like sand through a sieve
> And all too soon they've up and grown
> And then they've flown
> And it's too late for you to give ...[12]

N is for Nappy Rash and Nits

Nappy rash

Most babies get nappy rash at some point and it can be quite miserable dealing with it. My little ones always get sore bottoms when they are cutting teeth. Change nappies frequently, using cotton wool, water and baby lotion instead of babywipes. A bath after a dirty nappy can help enormously when they are sore. Pat the area dry, rather than rubbing, then let the air dry the little bottom completely. If your child is not yet moving around, give them some nappy-free time on the floor, lying on a changing mat and towel. When you need to put their nappy back on, apply a thick layer of Sudocrem first.

While we are on the subject of nappies, first-time mothers may appreciate a warning that newborn boys often urinate into the air (or your face) when you change their nappy during

12 'A man has dreams,' *Mary Poppins* (Walt Disney, 1964).

the first few weeks. For some reason the fresh air makes them go! Have a muslin cloth on hand to cover them while you are cleaning their backside. Older babies can sometimes make things difficult by getting their hands in the way during a nappy change. Giving them a small toy to hold can help.

Nits

The nursery school in our village has an almost permanent sign stuck on the front door announcing, 'THE NITS ARE BACK.' Basically, they never went away. I knew that it was only a matter of time before I would have to cope with the impossible combination of headlice and four daughters with curly hair. At the end of the summer holidays, every pharmacy in France is plastered with adverts for the latest miracle lice-killing potion. You'd be forgiven for thinking that the country is overrun with them. I even get adverts popping up on Facebook, promoting anti-louse hair salons that will hoover (yes, hoover) and comb your child's hair so that they are nit-free in just two sessions.

My eldest daughter had headlice once when she was about two years old. We bought a fantastic metal comb called a Nitty Gritty Nit Free Comb, easy to find in the UK in pharmacies and shops like Superdrug. These combs are sometimes named 'nit free terminator combs,' which sounds like something from a sci-fi film. (Have you seen a headlouse up close? Not pleasant. Getting itchy yet?) Terminator combs have long metal teeth with grooves in them and are much better than the flimsy white plastic ones. They are effective for removing all lice and eggs without the use of toxic (and often expensive) chemicals that may only destroy the live lice, not the nits (the eggs).

About three months ago I started getting an itchy head. I made my husband check me for lice … twice. He didn't find anything. I decided that I must have a strange pregnancy-induced allergic reaction to my shampoo. I bought some posh, pH-neutral, fragrance-free, everything-free, sensitive-scalp shampoo from a pharmacy, which didn't solve anything. I tried rubbing olive oil onto my head, leaving it on overnight and washing it off in the morning. Then I did the same with an anti-inflammatory cream. The itching was driving me crazy. Eventually I made an appointment with my doctor for the following week.

That evening at dinner time, I noticed my eldest daughter scratching her head and sure enough, there were lice scampering around (shudder). Out came the nitty gritty comb. I dreaded having to get it through curls, but if you wash the hair first, put on loads of leave-in conditioner and brush out the knots really well, it is possible. I found it helped to divide the hair into small sections so that I didn't have to drag the comb through a big bunch all at once. It also helped to keep the hair really wet. Lice often lay their eggs near the roots of the hair, on the crown of the head or around the ears, so it is good to go over those areas a few times. You can wipe the lice, nits and conditioner off into a tissue or piece of kitchen roll. That evening I spent three hours washing all my daughters' hair and using the special comb. They all had lice (and so did I, surprise surprise), but thankfully the other girls didn't have as many as their big sister, who was probably the one who brought them home from school. My husband and son amused themselves by cheering whenever a live louse was discovered and burning the used tissues on our concrete driveway.

I repeated the combing process after about three days and only found a few eggs that had been missed the first time … then repeated combing again after about a week to make sure that they had all gone. My third daughter is quite dramatic and hates having her hair brushed. The first time I used the nit comb on her she was sufficiently interested in what I might find to accept the occasional yank when it got stuck on a knot. The next time round I had to distract her with a cartoon. After using the comb, I also washed all our pillowcases and put the hairbrushes in the freezer overnight, since lice can survive for a day or so even if they are not on someone's head. I quickly cancelled my doctor's appointment, very glad that I had diagnosed the problem before he had to!

Some mothers recommend using special hair elastics infused with lice-repelling essential oils, such as tea tree and rosemary. These claim to provide protection for up to two months, but I doubt if they would persuade already-present headlice to move out.

O is for Online Shopping

One thing I love about France is the markets. Piles of seasonal fruit and vegetables, brightly coloured and bursting with flavour, the bustling crowds, the street cafés and the smell of fresh bread and coffee (yes okay, the markets also reek of fish and cheese and smelly dried sausages). I particularly love the markets in autumn, when the warm colours of falling leaves are reflected in the huge variety of pumpkins and other gourds. As much as I enjoy the atmosphere, it is rare that I venture to a market accompanied by small children. The pushchair gets stuck between crates, it takes too long to rummage around for one's purse in an enormous mummy handbag, and a child can disappear in the crowds in seconds while you are paying for a bag of oranges.

> Mum Diary: September 2015
> **Honesty**
> Y (age 4): 'Mummy, you smell of baguettes.'

In this season of life, I find online shopping an immense help. You can shop at any convenient moment during the day or night and it is easy to keep track of what you are spending. You can plan meals around whatever promotions are on that week. It also saves a lot of physical energy when compared to a trip to the supermarket—lugging your toddlers from the car to the trolley, keeping your children in check around the shop, putting groceries into the trolley, out again at the check-out, in again in bags, out again into the car and finally moving them from the car to the house. The bigger your family is, the more work this is! In the UK you can book home delivery slots in advance to get the cheap times. France hasn't quite caught on to home delivery yet, with the exception of certain pricey frozen goods shops, so we use the 'click and collect' service offered by many supermarkets, which is just as practical if we arrange to collect the food shopping on the way home from somewhere else.

P is for Potty Training

My mum told me that she potty trained my four siblings and me as soon as we turned two, and that it always took three weeks. I have often phoned her for moral support during this rather gruelling business. You can, of course, take the slower road of using 'feel wet' training pants. The problem with this is that little ones often don't actually feel wet, and therefore it can take longer for the whole process to click. I did use these for one of my children who was taking ages to get the hang of going to the potty for 'number twos.' She liked the fact that her 'nappy pants' had a ladybird picture on the front that disappeared if she had an accident. If you want to potty train the hard-core way and hopefully get it over and done with in three weeks, here are some steps to follow. Plan to start training when your child is about two years old, and preferably in the warmer months when you can be outside as much as possible and washing dries more easily. Try to leave your diary as empty as you can throughout the potty-training period.

Prepare in advance by:

1. Going out together to choose some big boy/big girl pants.
2. Practising sitting your child on the potty with or without clothes. Good times to do this are before they get in the bath or while you are on the toilet. (I mean, they follow you in there anyway, right?)
3. Talking about what the potty is for and how, very soon, they won't have to wear nappies any more.
4. If you have a slightly older, already potty-trained child, get them to demonstrate using the potty so that they can show their little sibling what to do.
5. Buying some colourful stickers.
6. Making a simple wall chart with the days of the week and space to stick a sticker for each success.
7. Rolling up any rugs that can be moved.
8. Moving to a house that has hard floors instead of carpets (only kidding, but seriously, potty training has been much easier on French tiled floors than it was in our fully-carpeted home near Manchester!).

When the big day arrives, brace yourself and put pants on your child. In cooler weather, tracksuit bottoms are also a good idea. They are quick to pull down and can soak up a lot of the inevitable accidents, which is better than having a huge puddle on the carpet. Set a timer to go off every 30 minutes. This is mostly to remind you to sit them on the potty regularly. Obviously, you eventually want them to start telling you when they need to go by themselves, but at the beginning they don't have a clue. By sitting them on the potty regularly, you have some hope of catching something. If you do catch something, let there be lots of clapping and celebration, and of course, a sticker on the chart. It can help to borrow extra potties from friends or your church so that there is always one nearby, as a reminder for everyone and so that you don't have to run so far.

One of my daughters was very reluctant to sit on the potty at all. I solved this problem by filling a cardboard box, known as 'the potty box,' with interesting toys, objects and books that she was only allowed to look at while sitting on the potty. Reading a little story on the potty can help to keep them there a bit longer. Expect a lot of accidents throughout the first week. Don't give up and above all, don't go back to nappies (but do continue to put them on for naps and nights). The accidents are all part of the learning process. At first little ones sometimes panic as they feel that unfamiliar trickle down their legs. They don't know that it is coming out of their body. Try not to get frustrated. Just tell them, 'It's okay. Never mind. We'll get you some clean pants. Next time, come and sit on the potty to do a wee. Look, here's the potty. Do your wee-wee here next time.'

With one of my children, day ten was a nightmare. We ran out of pants. To make matters worse, a lot of this happened in the creche room at church and various older ladies told me confidently that they didn't think she was ready. But she woke up on day eleven and it had suddenly clicked. She barely had a single accident after that. Another child took a full three weeks, but it wasn't stressful because she only made about three large puddles per day and most of those happened outside. One child was terrified of doing poos on the potty. Someone told me that lining the potty with an open nappy can help them feel less nervous about this! I can't remember if that worked or not, but she got there in the end. One of my worst memories of potty training is being in a DIY shop discussing paint colours with a shop assistant, when an awful smell began wafting up from the pushchair. I'll say no more.

For little boys' target practice, you can buy various specially-made floating objects that stay in the toilet bowl and don't flush away. Some even change colour! It is normal for children to regress a little at times during the training period, after they seemed to be getting the hang of things. Don't panic, just persevere! Expect the occasional accident throughout the coming year too. For this reason it is a good idea to put a pull-up nappy on your child for long car journeys. It is not much fun when your newly-trained child is desperate to go but the next motorway service station is miles away. Saving some pull-up nappies for travelling helps you all not to panic.

When you do have to go out during the training process, line the pushchair or car seat with a plastic bag and towel, head for parks or places with tiled, easy-to-clean floors, and don't forget to decorate the pushchair handles with hundreds of plastic bags containing the potty, spare clothes, water, wipes and more plastic bags to put the dirty clothes into. I know, it's a nightmare, but so worth the trouble once your child is nappy free!

Confession time: A couple of months after writing the above, confident that I had this potty-training thing sorted, I began training my fifth child. At first all went well. In just four days she was running to the potty by herself on time. But after three weeks of success she began going backwards, seeming not to care any more about being wet. Some days were literally full of poo. I couldn't blame my husband for putting pull-ups on her while I was in hospital after having baby number six. So, we are now back to square one and will have to repeat the process all over again in a few months. Which just goes to show that, as I said in the introduction, children are all different and what works for one may not work for another!

Q is for Questions

Children are naturally inquisitive. There is so much to learn. My son tends to bombard me with questions at breakfast time. 'What makes clouds move? How do they make glass? Why are mountains so big?' he asks, spreading Nutella on his toast and looking at me with serious dark eyes. Celebrate your children's curiosity! I have started looking for factories to take my inquisitive son to. In the meantime, YouTube videos are great for learning how people make things. We recently watched a fascinating one on how rubber gloves are made!

> ✎ Mum Diary: October 2014
> **Curiosity**
> Y (age 3), watching dad cutting his toenails:
> 'Did your feet growed in the night Papa?'

It is also important for you to ask your children questions. Not just simple questions that they can answer with monosyllables, but leading questions that will encourage them to open their hearts to you. So instead of asking, 'How was school today?' which will receive the inevitable answer, 'Fine,' you could ask, 'What was the best thing that happened to you at school today?' Or 'Did anything happen to make you sad at school today?' Really listening to your children's answers and responding with love and interest will help to form strong bonds of trust and security within your family.

R is for Routines

I am reluctant to say much about newborn routines. There is a lot of heated debate about demand versus schedule feeding. As I said in the introduction, what you decide to do is not a question of right and wrong. Every mother is different, and every baby is different. What works well for one child may not work for another. Bottle fed babies may take to a routine more naturally and quickly than breastfed babies, because you know approximately how much they need in each 24-hour period and you can see how much they are drinking. With the birth of each of my children I have become increasingly relaxed about feeding in general. I do believe that trying to get my first child to conform to a simple routine from the beginning (because of a book I read) was a bad idea, leaving her under-nourished and burdening me with false guilt when I didn't stick to it.

What I have found is that breastfed newborns tend to set their own evolving routine. For the first twelve hours or so after the birth, they tend to be sleepy and quiet. Then they start getting hungry and want to feed incessantly for two days. Go with it! Feed lying down if possible, so you can rest at the same time. Your milk will normally take three to four days to come through, although you do make nutrient-rich colostrum before that. The more you let your baby feed, the faster your breasts will start filling up and the happier your baby will be. Feeding a lot in those early days can also stop your breasts becoming painfully engorged with milk. Once your milk comes in properly, you will probably find that your baby gradually goes from feeding all the time, to feeding every one-and-a-half hours. As their tummy grows over the next few weeks the space between feeds will increase to two hours, then three. Every day is different. Your baby may need more feeds on hot days or days when his feeds keep getting interrupted by an inquisitive older sibling. Maybe he is distracted by noisy builders, or you only had time to give him half a feed before you had to go and get his sister from school. Sometimes babies just have hungry days (like you do!) and will want to feed a lot. It is also normal for babies to get fussy and want a lot of feeds at certain times of the day.

It can be difficult to stick to any kind of routine when you are breastfeeding a newborn baby. Some people refer to the first three months as the 'fourth trimester' of pregnancy, because your baby needs you so much. After that, however, things usually start getting a bit easier. Introducing flexible routines can be helpful for the whole family. Regular bedtimes, naptimes and mealtimes can help little ones to be settled and happy. It is useful to introduce a daily bedtime routine quite early in your baby's life, perhaps including a story, cuddles and prayers.

Children's routines will keep changing as they get older. You feel life has settled down, then they stop needing their morning nap, for example, and you have to adjust to a new schedule. There is security in routines that comes from knowing what to expect. God has built rhythms into the universe—seasons that come and go predictably, day and night, six days to work and one day to rest. He gave the Israelites regular festivals and events to mark the passing of time. We reflect his love of order when the hours we keep are not totally chaotic. Of course, there will be times when you break with your normal routine for a special occasion, when you are travelling, or because it is just such a beautiful summer evening that you can't possibly send the children to bed at the usual hour! The very existence of a normal routine that you can go back to is what makes these special occasions both physically bearable and enjoyable for all.

S is for Screens

It isn't good for anyone to have the TV on all the time and children will start to ignore it as background noise. Keep TV time for moments when they are out of sorts and tired or when you really have to get something done. I think most British mums are hugely thankful for a bit of calm provided by CBeebies! Conditional screen time can be useful as your children get older: 'Okay, you can watch TV, but only when your room is tidy, you have fed the hamster and finished your homework.' Be careful about what you allow your children to watch. Encourage them right from the start to love 'whatever is true, whatever is honourable, whatever is just, whatever is pure, whatever is lovely, whatever is commendable, [excellent] ... [or] anything worthy of praise' (Philippians 4:8). It is good, occasionally, to talk about things they see. 'Was that little girl kind to her brother? How could she have reacted differently? How do you think God would feel about that action or how that person is dressed?' We cannot escape from screens these days, so it is vitally important to teach your children to process the things they see on screens from a biblical perspective. Asking questions like this can help you to do that, as can talking about why you don't believe that a certain programme is appropriate for them.

> Mum Diary: May 2017
> **Current Affairs**
> Dad: 'You already know the Bible story we're going to read today, so I want you to guess who it's about. Here's a clue: A Jewish girl who became queen.'
> Y (age 6): 'Marine Le Pen?'

Keep screens in public places and especially keep them out of bedrooms. You need to know what your child is looking at and who they are communicating with, particularly if and when they start using the Internet. Make rules about screen-free times in your house right from when your children are little, rather than springing guidelines on them when this becomes more of an issue in the teenage years. For example, no screens at the table because we want to talk to each other, and no screens after a certain time in the evening, so that everyone can get a good night's rest. Interactive tablets are more stimulating than television, and so they are probably best avoided when preparing for naps or bedtimes. Make sure you obey these rules yourself to set a good example! One mother told me that letting her children play on a tablet when they are tired actually makes their behavior worse. Find what works for your family and control screen time to make life easier, rather than letting screens control you!

T is for Teething, Tummy Bugs and Tantrums

Teething

Some babies suffer a lot more than others when their little teeth start trying to poke through. Other than a lot of dribbling, getting bad nappy rash, and occasional grumpiness that was quickly solved with Calpol, my children thankfully seemed to have an easy time of it. However, this period can be difficult for many little ones and their parents. There are lots of types of teething rings out there, including some that you can put in the fridge or freezer so that the cold soothes little gums. Similarly, you can freeze bits of banana and other fruit for them to munch on. The following list of helpful medicines was taken from Facebook exchanges between my mummy friends:

- Ibuprofen for its anti-inflammatory effect
- Bonjela
- Dentinox Teething Gel
- Nelson's Teetha Teething Granules
- Other arnica teething granules
- Anbesol Teething Gel or Liquid—this was by far the most commonly recommended product by friends.

> Mum Diary: May 2016
> **Boys will be boys!**
> Today we read about Jim Elliot and his friends, missionaries who were speared to death by an Indian tribe in the jungles of Ecuador. L said, 'When I grow up, I want to be a missionary.' Y (age 5), eyes shining, said, 'When I grow up, I want to be an Indian.'

Some parents recommend jewellery made from amber stones. I have always been suspicious when people talk about the healing properties of stones. It sounds rather pagan. There is an idea that when in contact with body heat, amber releases minute amounts of oils that help with teething.[13] However, this has not been scientifically proven, and doctors generally warn against putting jewellery on babies because of the obvious choking and strangulation hazards.

Tummy bugs

Gastro enteritis is a mum's worst nightmare, especially if you catch it too while having to care for everyone else! Older children can aim into a bowl or the toilet, but it is especially difficult when babies and toddlers are sick as they tend to push a bowl away crossly and vomit over everything else. You

13 www.whattoexpect.com/first-year/ask-heidi/amber-teething-necklaces.aspx

can sometimes sit a bigger baby or toddler in the highchair, wearing a lipped silicone bib, during the worst period of vomiting, so that the bib catches the sick, though of course if your child feels very unwell, they may need to be on your lap or lying down. Move as many things out of their bed as possible (cuddly toys, extra blankets, etc.) to minimise clean up, and keep that washing machine going! Disposable bed mats, designed for bed-wetters, can also be handy for protecting sheets when a toddler is ill.

When a child has been throwing up and can't keep anything down and you really don't want them to eat but they are moany and hungry, fruit-flavoured ice pops are a good solution. Ice pops keep them hydrated and give them a bit of sugar to boost their mood. The child is also chuffed that they get to eat ice pops while everyone else has to have dinner. If your child won't drink rehydration fluids you can freeze these too to turn them into lollies. My doctor friend recently gave me a recipe for rehydration fluids, which is cheaper than buying them: 1 litre water, 8 tsp sugar, ½ tsp salt, ½ cup orange juice. Just mix it all up. Last time I had an upset stomach I sipped on this throughout the day and felt much more able to continue with normal responsibilities. Another tummy bug tip: Close the toilet lid before flushing sick away. Apparently, it stops germs flying around in tiny water particles and spreading to everyone else. Then of course, be liberal with disinfectant and remember that these times, whilst exhausting and horrid, usually don't last very long!

Tantrums

Although this book is not primarily about discipline issues, tantrums are such a prominent feature in the lives of many toddlers that they deserve a mention. I have recently noticed that there seem to be two types of toddler tantrum. Younger toddlers have times when their emotions are quite simply out of control and they don't appear to remember what made them upset in the first place. They scream, kick and throw themselves around. My twenty-month-old does this quite regularly at the moment. I find that what she needs most is a great big cuddle, and to be held firmly and lovingly until the storm of emotion subsides and we can go on to the next thing.

Then there is the second type of tantrum, in which an older toddler knows exactly what he or she wants and has decided to make as much fuss as possible until they get it. I only remember my oldest daughter having one of these. She threw herself down in the snow and kicked and screamed because she didn't want to leave the park. My second daughter has a gentle, compliant nature. I don't think she has even had a tantrum in her dreams. And then our son was born. Oh yes. One day I told the ladies at church that I feared I was raising a monster. He went through a phase of having five or six major tantrums every day when he couldn't have what he wanted. I remember trying to put him back into his pushchair outside the nursery school, after collecting his sister. Screaming and tummy pushing, body stiff as a plank. Unbendable. (This is another reason you need to exercise—you need to be stronger than your strong-willed two-year-old.) I finally clipped the pushchair buckle closed and looked up sheepishly at another mother who was standing nearby, casually watching me and smoking. 'Don't worry, I have the same at home,' she said, wryly.

The most embarrassing tantrum happened when I was in a health food shop buying oats, which at that stage were difficult to find in normal French supermarkets. Bird song music filtered sweetly through the sound system. People were calmly buying their soy milk and ecological washing powder. My son decided he wanted one of the expensive organic chocolate bars on display near the till. I said 'No,' and off he went. The queue was long, but it seemed like an eternity before we got out of the shop.

There is only one way to deal with this sort of tantrum: *Never give in.* Say quietly and firmly, 'Mummy said no. You will not get what you want by kicking and screaming.' You are the boss. You know what is best for your child. Don't give in, even when you feel like everyone in the shop is staring at you wondering if you or your child (or both) are crazy. This is very much a case of 'short-term pain for long-term gain.' Jesus knows all about this, and on a much larger scale. Ask him for help. The book of Hebrews says that 'for the joy that was set before him [Jesus] endured the cross, despising the shame, and is seated at the right hand of the throne of God' (Hebrews 12:2). Giving in to tantrums for the sake of short-term peace would lead, in the long run, to spoilt children who think they are entitled to whatever they like, whenever they like, if they just make enough fuss. Apparently, I had some of these tantrums myself. My parents once had to hold my bedroom door shut while I was inside raving. It took my son over a year to realise that the tantrums didn't get him what he wanted. During this year I wondered if *not giving in* was really having any effect at all. Of course, there were times when other types of discipline were also necessary. I am pleased to say that he is now a polite, friendly six-year-old who hasn't had a tantrum for many years. He laughs when I tell him how he used to make such a scene. Don't give up hope! Children go through phases. Sometimes they grow out of things without you doing much at all!

U is for Upside-Down Mattress Protectors

Fitted waterproof mattress protectors tend to be double-sided, with an impermeable layer underneath and a soft side which is clearly meant to be uppermost. I find it better to put them on upside down, waterproof side up. The seams look wrong, but they are covered by the sheet. You can then simply wipe the waterproof layer clean after accidents, instead of having to wash the whole thing. Keep mattress protectors that are ripped in the middle or no longer as waterproof as they once were. You can put them on top of a good mattress protector, under the sheet, as an extra layer to absorb accidents.

V is for Verrucas

Children are more likely than adults to pick up verrucas, because they are caused by a virus which one eventually becomes immune to. I remember the unpleasant experience of having verrucas frozen off at the doctor's surgery. Not wanting to make my daughter go through the same thing, I tried every natural remedy that I could find on the Internet on her verruca, including garlic, vinegar and oregano oil. None of these worked. What did work was a cream containing salicylic acid that I bought from the pharmacy. You put it on every evening and cover the area with a plaster. Within a couple of weeks the verruca just falls off. Duct tape is another solution worth trying if you can find a way to make it stay on. Stubborn verrucas may, however, need treatment by a doctor or dermatologist.

W is for Weaning

Your health visitor or doctor will advise you on when your baby is ready to start solid food. This is one area where medical advice keeps changing and people have many different ways of doing things. You may want to start by mixing a bit of baby rice with your child's usual milk. It is important for babies not to have gluten before they reach six months, as it can cause allergies. 'Baby-led weaning' is popular at the moment, which is basically where you start giving your baby bits of your own food. Other people still prefer the more traditional fruit and vegetable purées. I have always found that a combination of purées and finger foods works well. The advantages of liquidised food are 1. you can see what the baby actually eats, 2. feeding time is faster and less messy, and 3. the smooth consistency is easier for little gummy mouths to cope with. It takes a while for babies to get used to taking food off a spoon. During the first week or so they spit a lot of food right back out!

> Mum Diary: November 2017
> **Operation**
> This evening I had to use tweezers to take a piece of sweetcorn out of K's nose.

Babies love finger foods but a large proportion will end up on the floor or in their hair so it can be hard to know exactly what is being swallowed. It is, however, pure joy to watch your baby sucking on a whole strawberry, munching on a piece of toast or exploring the texture of a cooked carrot stick.

At the beginning, it can be useful to liquidise a batch of steamed or boiled vegetables and freeze little portions in silicon ice cube trays. Once they are frozen solid, you can transfer them to a freezer bag. I like to do several batches of individual vegetables, so I have an assortment of colourful vegetable cubes ready in the freezer. Root vegetables such as carrots, sweet potato and swede tend to go down well. Green vegetables such as broccoli and green beans are also good. Some doctors suggest introducing foods one by one so that you can see clearly if any new food upsets their tummy or causes a reaction. Once your baby has tried the vegetables separately you can start combining colours and flavours. Baby rice is hard to find in France, so I sometimes use dried potato granules for instant mash to thicken any vegetable purées that turn out too runny. You can gradually start to add meat and cheese into the mix. Fruit purées or fromage frais make good desserts. Your baby will start dropping milk feeds slowly and naturally as he takes in increasing amounts of solid food. You can offer water in a lidded beaker along with meals.

Once your baby tastes sweet foods, she may well start to turn up her nose at the more savoury flavours. One sneaky way to get babies to open their mouths for vegetables is to alternate spoonfuls of sweet and savoury foods so that they never know which to expect, but perhaps I should not encourage such underhand methods of baby deception! It certainly is a useful trick when you are in a rush and it gets the good stuff down them. Another way to get babies to open their mouth when they won't eat something, is to give them a second spoon to hold. I think this makes them think that they are feeding themselves.

When you first start introducing solids, a little bib tied round their neck is all you should need. I like to use soft white ones at first. Soft because the big plastic ones don't look comfortable on six-month-olds. White because carrot makes fantastic stains and if they are white you can spray bleach on them before washing. (Other coloured bibs do the trick too—it's only a bib—who really cares about stains?!) Once little ones start wanting to feed themselves, I find double-bibbing useful because babies put food everywhere. First you put on a long-sleeved machine-washable bib which covers their whole front and protects their sleeves. Then you put on a more rigid plastic or silicon bib with a lip that catches the dropped lumpy bits. I'm afraid there's not much you can do about babies rubbing food in their hair ... except take cute photos of hairstyles created by apple purée gel and send them to the grandparents.

Sometimes babies get very excited about eating and bat the spoon whenever it gets near their mouth. One way to avoid this is to sit them on your knee with one of their arms tucked under your side. Use your hand on the same side to hold their other hand while you feed them. Incidentally, this is also a useful position for cleaning the teeth of uncooperative toddlers. You just have to watch out for when they turn their face and wipe their mouth on your clothes.

My babies have always been eager for food from about five-months-old, watching us hungrily at mealtimes and sometimes even crying. I know other mothers whose babies do not show the slightest bit of interest in solids until much later. Don't worry too much about this. Keep an eye on their weight, mention it to your doctor or health visitor if you are concerned, and persist in offering little bits of food, particularly at family mealtimes. They will eventually become interested!

X is for XXX (Kisses!)

Your children need to know that they are loved. Showing physical affection comes more easily to some people than others and is certainly very natural and necessary when your children are little babies and toddlers. But even older children need to feel cherished. Take time for cuddles and kisses, lullabies, piggy backs and bedtime stories. Keep your relationship with your children warm and strong by showing appropriate physical signs of affection. They are more likely to accept correction with open hearts if they know that you really are on their side.

Y is for Yes

As a general rule, I try to say 'yes' to my children's requests whenever possible. I'm not talking about being child-centred, or spoiling them by giving them everything they ask for, but if they want to go somewhere or do something that is in line with biblical standards, why cause a battle or send them into a rebellious sulk thinking that 'Mum never lets me do anything,' simply because what they want to do is not convenient for me or not what I am in the mood for? Being affirmative and positive whenever possible allows you to pick your battles. When you do say 'no' to something, they will realise that there is a good reason for it and will be more likely to respect your explanation. This is something that becomes increasingly relevant as your children get older and start to make more decisions for themselves. They need to learn to analyse, not just what they see on screens, but also places, situations and activities, through a biblical lens. When you do say 'no,' use Scripture to show them why you don't think a certain activity would be honouring to God or beneficial for them. But don't become a miserable, restrictive mother who often says no to legitimate things, just because you can't be bothered! It will only lead to resentment and rebellion. Be a mother who usually says 'yes' and celebrates her children's interests.

> Mum Diary: January 2011
> **Ambition**
> L (age 3): 'Look, a moon! I want to touch it.'
> Mum: 'It's very far away.'
> L: 'Stand on a chair?'

Z is for ZZZ (Sleep)

I have yet to meet a parent of young children who doesn't wish that they could get a bit more sleep. You can expect various degrees of sleep deprivation throughout the first three months with a new baby, and sometimes for much longer. I remember sitting with my firstborn during long December nights, yearning for sunrise. It was quite a bit easier with my May babies. I don't have any magic solutions for getting a good night's sleep, but I can share a few tips that have helped us over the years.

Newborns frequently have their days and nights all mixed up. It can be tempting to let them sleep for hours during the day so that you can get things done, but you'll regret it that evening! There are ways to help babies get their days and nights the right way around. During the first two or three months, don't let your breastfed baby sleep for longer than three hours without a feed in the daytime. I tend to keep this up until the baby starts sleeping for longer stretches at night. If they have slept for three hours during the day, wake them up, let there be plenty of light, music or talking so they know that this is the time to eat and play. In the night when they wake for feeds, keep everything as dark, quiet and boring as possible. When babies need a nappy change during the night, it is a good idea to change them in the middle of their feed, rather than beforehand when they are

> Mum Diary: June 2016
> **Torture?**
> Nights with a newborn can sometimes feel like a form of torture. You don't let someone sleep until most of the night is gone anyway, then for the next few hours whenever they fall asleep you keep waking them up and screaming at them. I'm glad this doesn't last forever, and also that every night is not as bad as last night was!

hollering with hunger, or afterwards, when it may wake them up too much just when you want them to settle again. Changing the baby mid-feed can also help to keep them awake for the second half of their meal, so that they drink more and hopefully sleep a bit longer.

Another thing I have found useful is recognising the first signs of tiredness and putting the baby down for a nap or to bed immediately. You can even put them down for a nap before they start getting tired if you know that they have been awake for a while. Once babies get overtired, they have a much harder time settling.

Small babies love sleeping close to mum and quickly recognise the difference between being all cosy in mum's bed for a feed, and then suddenly transferred to their cold, lonely moses basket. The benefits and problems of co-sleeping can be read about all over the Internet, so I won't discuss them here. There have been hundreds of times when I have finished feeding baby in the late evening, baby falls asleep, I gingerly try to put baby in his own bed without waking him up … all to no avail! One solution is to put a hot water bottle in your baby's bed while he is having his feed. Feed him already swaddled in cosy blankets or a baby sleeping bag, which will not have to be moved when transferring him, then remove the hot water bottle just before you put baby down. This does not always work, but sometimes babies relax into the warmth and stay asleep, which means you can go to sleep too. Yesss!

For older children aged two and up, a Gro-clock can be a wonderful solution to being woken very early in the morning. These are special clocks that show a blue star face during the night, which then changes to a sunshine face in the morning at your chosen time. Children can quickly learn that they mustn't get out of bed or make a noise until the sunshine appears on the clock. Black-out curtains can also help children to sleep for longer during the summer months. Here in France we have shutters which are so effective that English visitors often oversleep because it is so dark!

Epilogue

Heart pounding, I rushed into the empty street. No one to the right. No one round the corner. A neighbour drove by and stopped when she saw the look on my face. 'Are you okay?' 'I've lost K,' I answered, my mouth dry. The first thing I had done was check the paddling pool. There was no way she could climb in there anyway—the sides are too high for two-year-old legs to get over, but still, better safe than sorry. Then I checked the two garden gates that lead onto the street. Both closed. I reasoned that she couldn't open the gates, and even if she had gone into the street, she would surely have left them open. Phew, she must be here somewhere then. 'Come out now if you're hiding. It's not funny anymore!' I had called.

My older girls had checked under all the beds and in all the cupboards while I scoured the garden again. No sign of her. 'If she's not in the house or garden and the gates are closed, then someone must have come in and taken her away. Oh Lord, help! My beautiful baby girl.' That was when I rushed into the street. My neighbour pulled over and said she would walk around the estate to look for her while I continued to search the house. Should I call the police? My husband? Where should I start? Should I leave the other children by themselves and go out to look for her? What about my newborn baby who was halfway through a feed when her sister disappeared? I imagined my precious toddler held down in the back of the car of some horrid child trafficker. Pain and panic ripped through me as the seconds ticked by.

Another lady who lived further up our road stopped her car outside our house and wound the window down. 'I think I've just seen your daughter in the road. I nearly ran her over when I backed out of my drive. You should be more careful.' Ignoring her implied criticism and wondering why she hadn't picked my daughter up and brought her to me, I was about to run up the road, when a third lady from the neighbourhood appeared around the corner, carrying K in her arms. Such a relief! I remained tearful and trembly for several hours. My two-year-old had opened the heavy garden gate, closed it silently behind her and wandered happily up the street in pyjamas and bare feet. It goes without saying that we have kept the gates locked from then on. For a couple of weeks following the incident I wondered if the disapproving lady who nearly ran my daughter over was going to report us to social services for letting two-year-olds wander around in the road.

Moments like this remind us just how much we love our children, no matter what everyday hassles they may cause. We would die for them. Love is the ultimate force which enables us to press on and thrive as mothers. Love enables us to meet our children's needs. Love hopes when no one else does. Love gives us strength to serve when we are already exhausted. Here is one mother's paraphrase of the 'love verses' in 1 Corinthians 13:

> Though I lecture and harp at my children and have not love, I will be background noise to rebellious thoughts.

And though I wisely warn them not to use the street as a playground, or they'll be killed; and though I patiently explain why snails live in mobile homes, and I give endless answers to life's other mysteries; and though I have faith that can remove mountains of ignorance—yet never hug my children—I have taught nothing.

And though I slave over a steaming stove with balanced diets and complicated recipes and even burn my fingers—yet never smile as I serve—I have not really fed them.

A truly loving mother suffers through unfinished sentences, clutter, nicks on furniture, sleepless nights, and adolescent insults, and is kind enough to think her kids are the greatest. A loving mother tries not to resent her children for being free like she used to be, and she doesn't brag about how she never talked to her mom that way.

Real love: considers a childish nightmare more urgent than her need for sleep; is not shattered by the title "Meanest Mom"; doesn't shame a toddler who breaks training or a teen who still spills milk; steadfastly refuses to entertain visions of escape; and does not smirk as her child trips over the toy he refused to put away (but with silent wisdom rejoices in the effective lessons of experience).

Mother-love has arms strong from lifting, a heart large with believing, a mind stretched with hoping, shoulders soft with enduring, and knees bent with committing.

> True mother-love never fails to point her child to the Author of Love.[14]

Human love is frail. We cannot love our children like this in our own strength. We need to be filled with Divine love so that we can, in turn, pour that love out on our children. 'We love because he first loved us' (1 John 4:19).

We also need to entrust our children to God's love. This is the key to having a peaceful heart, no matter how old our children are. I recently read an article by a mother who struggled with postnatal anxiety. While mental illness clearly played a role in her experiences, her battle was ultimately caused by the false belief that 'I am the only one who can protect my children.' Learning to entrust our children's lives to the One who created them and loves them more than we ever could, will prevent our love from becoming grasping, suffocating for our children and worry-inducing for us. When I got married, ladies from three churches put together a little book for me, in which each of them had written some words of advice or encouragement. My mum's contribution ended with these words: 'In good times (and *very* good times), in bad times (and *very* bad times), the right thing to do is always the same … continue trusting God and continue obeying him.'

So, fellow mums, take the time to look after your own mental, physical, spiritual and social health. I hope that some of the practical tips in this book will help you to thrive in motherhood. Entrust yourself and your children to the care of our almighty God, who is Love.

14 Susan L. Lenzkes, *When the Handwriting on the Wall is in Brown Crayon*, Marshall Pickering, 1988

One cloud remains, that by your birth
You're entering a ruined earth,
My little one.

But you shall find with sweet surprise
Earth but a pathway to the skies,
My little one.

Such is our trust, for, Lord, we give
Your gift to you! O then receive
Our little one.

Receive her, Lord, and let her be
Your own to all eternity—
Your little one.[15]

15 H. Grattan Guinness, 19th century. I have updated the thees and thous! This poem was read out at the dedication service for our second child.

Appendix 1: Tips for older women (and others) who want to help young mothers

I have been blessed by the help and advice of older women at many different times. The book of Titus encourages older women to teach younger ladies to 'love their husbands and children, to be self-controlled, pure, working at home, kind, and submissive to their own husbands, that the word of God may not be reviled' (Titus 2:4–5). Sometimes this will take place in a formal mentoring relationship. Usually, however, this sharing and learning takes place naturally as we 'do life' together.

Younger women can learn so much from those who have walked a similar path before them. This requires both parties to have a certain willingness to be vulnerable. Sharing struggles, burdens and failures takes humility. Letting older ladies into our messy homes so that they can help us to clean them can be difficult, but when we are willing to peel away the mask of our public image, it can lead to deeper relationships and many great blessings. Since this type of relationship requires realism and openness, it has to be built on trust. Trust often comes when we seek to serve and help others in practical ways. We often want to help people but are not sure how to go about it. Sometimes we are scared of seeming pushy and interfering. No one wants to come across as a busybody. Simply saying, 'Let me know if I can help,' is good, but often not enough to persuade the person to call on you when in need. So, to give you some ideas of how to begin, here are some specific ways in which older ladies have helped me and opened the door for meaningful exchanges and opportunities for me to learn from them. I would like to help other young mothers in the same way, as my children and I get older…

Let's start with the negative: What not to say to a mother with small children

1. *'Small children, small problems, big children, big torments.'* Older French ladies *love* saying this. There is no doubt some truth in the statement, but I find it terribly depressing for two reasons: 1) It belittles the struggles that mothers of small children are having now and the exhaustion they often face. 2) It offers a bleak view of the future. Jesus told us not to worry about tomorrow. Being encouraged to worry about driving tests and car crashes and teenage pregnancies and exposure to drugs and alcohol is not helpful when you are already struggling with a teething baby and a three-year-old who has seven tantrums a day.

2. *'When my children were little, I always made sure the house was spotless by the time my husband came home'* or *'Cleanliness is next to godliness.'* If you say things like this the young mother may be terrified to invite you round and will live in fear of you dropping in unexpectedly. Remember that the mother may be working her socks off all day long and still have

a messy house. Trying to tidy and clean while you have small children is a bit like shovelling snow while it is still snowing. Don't pile on the guilt by making statements about how orderly your house and life have always been.

Positive ways to help and encourage a young mother

1. *Speak encouraging words.* Compliment her on something specific that she is doing well or on something good that you see in her children. She doesn't often hear people affirming her in her role.

2. *Love the children.* Greet the children by name and show an interest in their lives.

3. *Ask the mother how you can pray for her*—then remember to do so. Could you offer to meet with her regularly to pray?

4. *Offer to look after her little ones in the creche* one Sunday at church, so that she can focus on the sermon for a change.

5. *Turn up at the door with a home-cooked meal.*

6. *Ask to take a bag of ironing home with you.*

7. *Turn up with tools and gloves and do the gardening.*

8. *Equip your house to have young families round.* Hide the china, buy some plastic plates and cups, a high chair and a few toys. That is all it takes to make young families feel welcome.

9. *Give the mother a small amount of money and tell her that she must spend it on a treat for herself.*

10. *Ring her as you are going out to the supermarket* to ask

if there is anything she needs that you could buy while you are there and then drop round.

11. *Take the children out for a few hours* to give the mother time to get things done at home or so that she can rest. This offer will be especially welcome when she is preparing to travel or is going through a busy period.
12. *Offer to babysit* so that she and her husband can go out for a meal or so that she can get her hair cut, etc.
13. *Ask, 'Can I come over one day this week to help you at home? Write me a list of jobs to do and I'll do them.'*
14. *Share your own struggles as a mother and what helped you.*
15. *Buy her this book!*

Appendix 2: Recommended resources

Christian Parenting

Aren't They Lovely When They're Asleep: Lessons in Unsentimental Parenting by Ann Benton (Christian focus, 2007). This is my favourite Christian parenting book—it is concise, down-to-earth, biblical and practical. By the way, I got the idea of using an A-Z structure from Lesson 2 in this book. Ann Benton's teaching has also been turned into an excellent course, with a DVD, Leader's Guide and Study Guide: *'Putting Parenting to Bed—Uncommon Sense for Modern Parents'* (The Good Book Company, 2009).

Parenting Collection—The New Dare to Discipline, The New Stong-Willed Child, Parenting isn't for Cowards by Dr James Dobson (Tyndale House Publishers, 2010).

Shepherding a Child's Heart by Tedd Tripp (Shepherd Press, 1995).

Biblical Womanhood

Disciplines of a Godly Woman by Barbara Hughes (Crossway Books, 2001).

God's Design for Women in an Age of Gender Confusion by Sharon James (Evangelical Press, 2019).

Lies Women Believe and the Truth That Sets Them Free by Nancy DeMoss Wolgemuth (Revived Hearts Foundation, 2018).

Spiritual Mothering—The Titus 2 Model for Women Mentoring Women by Susan Hunt (Crossway Books, 1992).

www.girltalkhome.com (It contains 'conversations on biblical womanhood and other fun stuff.')

www.reviveourhearts.com (Radio programmes and many other helpful resources.)

www.reviveourhearts.com/true-woman/blog/ (Helpful articles for women by a team of Christian bloggers.)

Devotionals for Mothers

New Baby Survival Guide, Bite-sized Bible Reading for New Mothers by Cassie Martin & Sarah Smart (The Good Book Company, 2013). I was given this as a gift when my sixth child was born, just after I finished writing this book. The spiral-bound format makes it great to hold while feeding a baby and the passages, comments, questions and tips are helpful. There is a brief A-Z of mothering tips at the end. I was pleased to see that my A-Z has the letters standing for different things, except 'z' for sleep …

Pressing Pause—100 Quiet Moments for Moms to Meet With Jesus by Karen Ehman & Ruth Schwenk (Zondervan, 2016). Amazon says, '*Pressing Pause* offers you a calm way to start your day, to refresh yourself in Jesus and drink deeply of His presence so that you are ready to pour out love, time, and energy into the people who matter most to you. These 100 encouraging devotions for moms will help you begin each day with Scripture, drawing on God's power, ingesting His Word, and learning practical ways to love and serve more like His Son.'

Marriage and Family

Feminine Appeal—Seven Virtues of a Godly Wife and Mother by Carolyn Mahaney (Crossway Books, 2003).

For Women Only by Shaunti Feldhaln (Multnomah, 2017).

Men, Women and Families by Elisabeth Elliott (Alpha, 1999).

What is a Family? by Edith Schaeffer (Baker Book House, 1975).

Hospitality and Home

A Cup of Cold Water by Julia Jones (Day One, 2006). This is a practical book on hospitality.

Decluttering at the Speed of Life by Dana K.White (Thomas Nelson, 2018).

Resources for Family Worship Times

A Book for Family Reading, volumes 1 and 2 by Jim Cromarty (Evangelical Press, 1995 & 1996), (age 4 and up). Interesting stories to teach biblical truths to the whole family, links to Scripture passages to read and discussion questions.

Everything a Child Should Know About God by Kenneth N. Taylor (10Publishing, 2014), (age 3–6). This is a bit like a systematic theology for little ones. It is really accessible and age appropriate with good illustrations and questions to ask to check that your child has understood.

First Virtues—12 Stories for Toddlers by Dr Mary Manz Simon (B & H Publishing Group, 2016), (age 2–5). Some of the rhymes are a bit forced, but otherwise a good book for toddlers.

God's Names by Sally Michael (P and R Publishing Company, 2011), (age 8–12).

*How a Spider Saved a Man's Life and 51 Other Great Stories (*52 Spurgeon Stories for Children) by Tony Hutter (Day One, 2011), (age 5–12).

Leading Little Ones to God by Marian M. Schoolland (William B Eerdman's Publishing Company, 1962), (age 4–11). This is another systematic theology for children. The discussion questions are good. Unfortunately, it uses 'thees and thous' for the little prayers at the end of each reading. It can sometimes be a bit moralistic and not as grace-based as one could wish.

The Beginner's Bible by Catherine DeVries (Mission City Press, 2005) and the *Beginning with God* Bible notes, available at www.goodbook.co.uk, (age 2–5). Toddlers love the format of these notes, especially the sticker part!

The Big Picture Story Bible by David Helm (Crossway, 2004), (age 2–7). This book is great for showing how the Bible is one big story of redemption, and how individual stories fit into the big picture.

The Child's Story Bible, volumes 1, 2 and 3 by Catherine F. Vos (first printed between 1934 and 1936 and reprinted many times since). Some of the language is a bit dated but it is still excellent. It covers the whole Bible.

The Jesus Storybook Bible by Sally Lloyd-Jones (Zondervan, 2007), (age 4–8). This is my favourite children's Bible. The stories are told in such a warm, living, Christ-centred way.

The Princess and the Kiss by Jennie Bishop & Susan Henson (Revive Our Hearts, 2004) and the companion study guide, *Life Lessons from the Princess and the Kiss* (age 6 to teen). This contains biblical teaching on purity, relationships and marriage in a format that really appeals to little girls, and is fantastic for mums to study with their daughters. *The Squire and the Scroll* is the boys' equivalent.

Other Resources to Read with Your Children

Growing up God's Way—for Boys (age 10–14) and *Growing up God's Way—for Girls* (age 9–14) by Dr Chris Richard and Dr Liz Jones (Evangelical Press, 2014). These are not suitable for family worship times, but are great books to read one-on-one with your pre-teen to prepare them for puberty in a biblical way.

Lies Girls Believe and the Truth That Sets Them Free by Dannah Gresh & Nancy DeMoss Wolgemuth (Moody Publishers, 2019), (age 9–12). This is an excellent book to help 'tweens'—and there is a mum's guide that goes with it: *A Mom's Guide to Lies Girls Believe* by Dannah Gresh & Nancy DeMoss Wolgemuth (Moody Publishers, 2019).

Other Helpful Websites

www.bounty.com and www.whattoexpect.com (Tips to do with pregnancy, childbirth and the toddler years.)

www.healthystart.nhs.uk (Information about vouchers for infant formula, milk, and fruit and vegetables.)

www.mothersathomematter.co.uk (An organisation that promotes the value of stay-at-home parents, seeking to influence politics and make the choice to stay at home financially possible for more people. The website features many interesting articles, for example, on the value of unpaid work at home according to national statistics, and the impact of an absent mum on the long-term emotional and mental wellbeing of children.)

www.nhs.uk (To search for and find advice on medical conditions.)

Facebook page 'Can I breastfeed in it?' (For ideas on which clothes work well for breastfeeding.)